10

Dilemmas in Child Custody

Family Conflicts and Their Resolution

Andrew P. Musetto

Nelson-Hall nh Chicago

LIBRARY OF CONGRESS CATALOGING IN PUBLICATION DATA

Musetto, Andrew P., 1945–
   Dilemmas in child custody.

   Bibliography: p.
   Includes index.
   1. Children of divorced parents. 2. Custody of children. I. Title
HQ777.5.M87   306.8'7   81-22579
ISBN 0-88229-736-8   AACR2

Manufactured in the United States of America

10   9   8   7   6   5   4   3   2   1

The paper in this book is pH neutral (acid-free).

CONTENTS

To Betty and Ruth and Jeanne and Stephanie

PREFACE

THIS BOOK IS A CLINICAL report based on my experience with families involved in child custody and visitation disputes. It is not a research effort, although the findings of researchers are involved. I espouse a particular point of view — namely, that a child custody or visitation dispute is a family problem, and that to be resolved it necessitates the active cooperation of the entire family. This has been my clinical approach since becoming involved in this area more than six years ago.

I hope this book will help divorcing or separating parents who agonize over the custody and visitation of their children. By understanding what is happening to them and their children, they may learn more constructive ways to resolve these problems instead of engaging in the bitter custody contests that are common today.

Adjusting to a separation or divorce is like adjusting to any other crisis in personal or family life. Issues must be faced, problems solved, new roles adopted, and old roles discarded. The aftermath of a divorce is similar to the time following the death of a loved one. Desensitization to the loss, grief, mourning, anger, and disengagement are necessary and salutary. Not every child is permanently damaged by a divorce, but each child is particularly vulnerable. I hope that this book helps prevent those vulnerabilities from becoming disabilities, those temporary hurts from becoming enduring conflicts. I will raise what I believe are the most important issues regarding child custody and visitation. I will also present methods of coping with and surviving a custody or visitation controversy.

A custody dispute over children inevitably has to do with the parents' marital relationship, each parent's personal identity and concrete situation in life, and how each parent adjusts to the separation or divorce. Direct and powerful is the relationship between a resolution to the marital relationship and how the custody or visitation problems are handled. Chronic, unresolved, acrimonious marital problems can be played out as custody or visitation controversies, even after the divorce decree has grown old.

Children have various reactions to a separation, divorce, and the problems of custody and visitation. Transitory disturbances are common. Seemingly normal, well-adjusted children begin to exhibit uncharacteristic behavior. They become withdrawn, apathetic, and they have trouble eating or sleeping. They revert to less mature behavior; they stop doing things that they were once able to do for themselves. They demand more attention and never seem to be satisfied. Angry outbursts and depression are typical.

Parents who read this book will possibly learn what to avoid to prevent their children from long, destructive entanglements in custody wars. I hope they will also gain a better sense of what they can do that is positive for their children and themselves as they separate and decide about custody and visitation. As separated or divorced parents read through this work they can be reassured: they are not alone in wondering and suffering over custody or visitation.

I have aimed this book at clinicians as well as parents. I have planned it to be serious enough to grasp the complexity of child custody issues, but not so technical as to be unintelligible to the average reader. It is not meant to be a cookbook, yet it contains specific advice and suggestions. It is not strictly speaking a scholarly book, but it includes considerable theory and abstraction. I hope it will be comprehensive enough to appeal to clinicians by offering them insights that they can use in their practices, but practical enough to be useable and helpful for parents. Perhaps, in addition, judges, attorneys, physicians, educators, and other professionals will gain a better grasp of the complexity and pain associated with custody and visitation dramas.

Mostly, I have written this book for the sake of children, for the many agonized and perplexed faces that I have witnessed in the last few years. If the frightening uncertainty that comes from not knowing what one's future will bring or if the turmoil that results from being trapped in the midst of parents' marital battles can be lessened for some children, this book will have hit its mark.

Various specific questions are asked here. What are children's most important needs during and after divorce and custody or visitation hearings? Who is responsible for a custody or visitation battle? Why do parents fight bitterly about custody or visitation? Whose needs and rights come first, parents' or children's? Why do children have such diverse reactions to divorce? Should a child be told about an impending separation, and if so, how? What happens to parents during a divorce and custody determination? What can they do to help themselves and their children adjust? Who should get custody? What about joint custody? Should mothers be favored over fathers? What happens during the evaluation and counseling of a family involved in a legal contest over custody or visitation? When should someone other than a biological parent be given custody? When is professional help needed, and how can it be used effectively? What are some of society's attitudes toward custody and visitation? What is the history of custody and visitation laws? How are they changing? What happens if one parent refuses to be involved with the children after a marital separation? What are possible legal solutions to custody and visitation contests?

I have tried to write not what is popular but what I think is true about the history and problems of child custody. No doubt many will understand the issues differently. My hope is that this work will be an invitation to dialogue, not a foreclosure of any subject. It should be a search for a close approximation of the reality of child custody issues, not simply a biased and ideological statement. Bias, however, has surely crept into my findings: the bias is one in favor of justice and fairness among family members, among generations, and ultimately among people.

The book is written with a developing perspective: early chapters are the foundation for later ones. Concepts such as justice, loyalty, and the family as a system are defined early and must be understood if later chapters are to make sense. The interlocking of four areas forms the theoretical framework of the book. Individual needs, personality and developmental characteristics, occur within a family, an organized, rule-governed system of relationships. These relationships can be trustworthy and growth-enhancing or lacking in trust and debilitating. Cultural attitudes and laws influence and are influenced by custody practices. The individual, the family, the relational, and the cultural-legal aspects must be grasped to understand what today's custody disputes are about.

I would like to say that this book is both original and borrowed. I owe a debt to many authors, and I hope it is clear where my debt lies. Some of the work is original, drawn from my own clinical experiences. Certain ideas were first published as articles (Musetto, 1978a, 1978b).

My colleagues at the Camden County Health Services Center in Lakeland, New Jersey, have helped me immeasurably. I thank them all. In particular I am grateful to David Cordier, M.A., and Lillian Scheiner, Ed.D., for reading my manuscript and offering constructive criticism. I especially thank Mary Cordier for typing my work.

ONE

Introduction

OURS IS AN AGE OF rapid change. Many of our religious, governmental, cultural, and social institutions have been deeply influenced by current trends. One such institution is the family. The soaring divorce rate reflects the turmoil that marriages and families are going through.

According to the U.S. census, in 1970 about one out of four marriages ended in divorce. In 1977, the figures rose to one out of three (Rohrlich, Ranier, Berg-Cross, and Berg-Cross, 1977). By most indications, the rate continues to increase. And these figures do not include permanent separations or desertions. The divorce rate in 1976 was 5.0 per 1,000 population, an increase of 7 percent from 1975. Taking her data from government sources, Everly (1977) reported that "this figure represents over 2,166,000 adults and over a million children and constitutes the most rapidly increasing type of single parenthood" (p. 7).

As divorces increase so does the number of children affected. More and more children are living in single-parent homes, or blended families, where one parent is a stepparent. As of 1976, one out of every six children under eighteen lived in a single-parent home. That represented 11 million out of 66 million children (Everly, 1977). It is no wonder that researchers and social scientists have turned their attention to the impact of divorce and separation on children.

1

This book addresses a particular facet of divorce and its impact on children: namely, child custody and visitation. Today, this is an especially important topic, not because every divorce damages a child, but because divorce places all children at a high risk of emotional harm. Custody battles greatly heighten this risk.

Divorce or separation does not necessarily end an emotional relationship. A custody or visitation dispute, usually a continuation of unresolved marital and family problems, signify that the marriage is not over emotionally. A clinician, parent, or researcher who wishes to understand, cope with, or resolve a custody or visitation dilemma must address the child's family, for it is the family conflicts that give rise to and sustain these problems, and it is only with the help and cooperation of the family that they can be worked out constructively.

This book is a report of my clinical efforts with families involved in custody and visitation disputes; it is not a research project. The theme of the book is that custody and visitation problems are family problems: all members of a family affect and are affected by custody and visitation disagreements. A resolution to a custody or visitation problem will be successful only if it engages the entire family, especially the parents.

Although painful and stressful for everyone, to children, divorce can be devastating, especially if while deciding about custody their parents put their personal needs ahead of the rights and interests of their children. Before trying to understand the reasons for these custody and visitation conflicts and possible solutions to them, the theoretical framework of the book will be explained. It will be restated directly and indirectly throughout the entire work.

THEORETICAL FRAMEWORK

Divorce is a transition in a family's life. A bitter, unresolved custody or visitation contest means that the transition has not been completed successfully. Unable to separate from each other emotionally, parents continue their unsettled problems through custody or visitation battles. Although not every custody suit is a reflection of parental failure to separate emotionally, many are. When custody suits do not reflect this failure to separate, parents realize quickly the devastating effects their fighting has on their children, and they can more easily set aside their grievances for the sake of their children.

The premise of this book (and my clinical work) is that disputed custody encompasses four levels: the individual, the family, the relational, and the cultural-legal, all of which must be understood to resolve custody conflicts. Individuals usually belong to families which shape personality and in which loyalty among family members is intrinsic, natural, and often hidden. A family is also a system that consists of many features, including communication patterns, roles and alignments between two or more people (sometimes against another family member), rules and expectations that govern and regulate behavior, typical and repetitive ways of solving problems, and degrees of distance and closeness among members.

But a family is not just a system, it is a system of relationships, and the quality of those relationships comprise the third level, what Boszormenyi-Nagy and Spark call relational ethics. Family relationships either encourage family members toward personal growth, or they exploit them. Those members who are neglected, abused, unwanted, discarded as burdens, continually criticized, ignored, overindulged, infantalized, or cut loose from the family prematurely are exploited and left with a "sense of injured justice" (Boszormenyi-Nagy and Spark, 1973) — the feeling of being treated unfairly. Being given too little, they go through life feeling entitled, demanding that others make up for what they missed. Those given too much feel indebted and spend their lives trying to do for others while neglecting themselves. The former believe the world owes them a living — as the saying goes — and the latter that they owe everyone, with no rights of their own. A healthy family strikes a balance between giving and receiving: it provides enough caring and guidance so that its members feel wanted and self-confident, but it expects each member to give something to the family in return, to treat the other members fairly and lovingly. People either grow in families, or they die there.

The result of unresolved marital and family problems and conflicting needs and interests between children and their parents, custody and visitation disputes sting parents and children alike, causing anxiety and uncertainty. Just as children have needs so parents have their own needs to meet. They have to disengage emotionally from their former spouses and begin a new life-style. Financial pressures can force them into the job market and compel them from part-time to full-time employment, often at necessary but unrewarding jobs. Reduced income curtails many activities. Inasmuch as the two-parent family still tends to be the ideal for our society, single parents are often lonely, isolated, and depressed. Their lives are in flux. Friends, and sometimes family members, can desert them. Guilt over a failed marriage or separation from their children colors their feelings. A painful period of uncertainty is usual, before they understand who they are and where they are going. Involved court battles increase their animosities instead of easing their burdens. Despite parents' problems, there are still the children, who need consistent, responsible parenting. Their parents may want to care for them responsibly but find themselves overwhelmed and emotionally depleted. Children require the security and stability of a loving relationship with a parent or caretaker, the very thing that may be most difficult to come by during an extended custody or visitation fight. Children need to be free of the harshness of uncertain, capricious futures that divorce and unresolved custody contests impose on them. They need to be liberated from involvement in their parents' marital and custody battles, so that trust, not fear, and hope, not despair, make up the fabric of their relationships.

Custody and visitation conflicts, therefore, are family problems. Children have individual needs, developmental tasks, and unique personalities. In the family to which a child belongs, these needs are either met and the child is encouraged to competence and maturity, or they are impeded and neglected and the child is prevented from growing emotionally. With a trusting relationship between a child and his or her parents, that child can be helped through a divorce and custody determination, despite the breakup of the family. On the other hand, the child who is used to trying to settle the parents' marital problems, or who is neglected because a parent is overwhelmed by the pressures of being divorced or single, is exploited and probably damaged.

Not only do unfinished marital problems, family relations, and the clash of individual needs affect custody, but also society's attitudes toward marriage, divorce, child-rearing, and child custody, expressed partially in laws, shape custody decisions. Although it cannot assure responsible parenting or change attitudes, the court's decision will affect who will have contact with the children and who should make important decisions regarding their lives—that is, who will have custody. The presence of financial stability and supportive friends and peers will greatly aid in adjustment to divorce or separation. Without both, adjustment will be more difficult, custody more conflictual, and children's needs more neglected. To complete the transition of divorce, to help parents disengage emotionally, to insure the rights and needs of children as well as their parents, to constructively decide child custody dilemmas, each of the four levels — the individual, the family, the relational, and the cultural-legal — as well as their interrelationships with each other, need to be understood.

FAMILY THERAPY

Since this work is based primarily on family therapy concepts, it is important to understand this theoretical and therapeutic approach to personal and relationship problems.

One of the most significant advances in mental health in the last thirty years, family therapy is truly a new idea; it locates the chief source of emotional problems in the interrelatedness among all family members and generations rather than within the internal makeup of a single individual or in a dyadic relationship between two people. The perspective of family therapy includes intrapsychic variables, but it puts them in a new context, gives them a new understanding, and sees them intimately and inextricably connected to family relationships. Family therapy calls our attention to patterns of relationships and sequences of events within a family more than to what goes on in the minds of each member. A mother turns to her eleven-year-old son, for example, whenever she feels depressed following an argument with her husband, the boy's father. The boy listens but feels burdened; he worries about his mother and blames his father. At school his attention drifts to his home life, and his school work suffers. The boy's academic problems draw his mother closer. Sensing the mother's closeness to the boy and distance from himself, the father withdraws to his work. The more he withdraws, the more she feels rejected and then turns to her son for companionship.

Regardless of which comes first, the father's withdrawal stimulates the mother's depression and enmeshment; her overinvolvement pushes the father toward the periphery of the family. Isolation and emotional distance, depression and enmeshment, and school problems fit together like a puzzle: no piece is completely understandable without reference to the others. In short, although diversified and nuanced by many schools of thought and approaches, family therapy means that we cannot fully understand a person apart from the interpersonal and family relationships in which that individual participates.

The family therapy movement began in the late forties and early fifties (Guerin, 1976). World War II had ended and the

Korean conflict was taking place. As a backlash to the disrupting family separations due to these wars, there was a great emphasis in American society on togetherness. Psychoanalysis was having its day in the field of mental health. Although well-established, it had its limitations: the genius of its founder, Sigmund Freud, had fallen into the dogmatism of many of his followers. Psychoanalysis in specific and psychiatry in general were frustrated on two fronts: working with schizophrenic families, and trying to change behavioral disorders and delinquency in children and adolescents.

In this context and partially out of these frustrations, family therapy was born. It began, as Guerin wrote (1976), as family research. Influenced by psychoanalytic principles, clinicians were afraid to violate the sanctity of the patient-therapist relationship by direct contact with a patient's family. The ideal of good therapy at the time was to have a psychiatrist work with the symptomatic family member, for example a child, while a social worker interviewed the parents. Later on, as preliminary family work was favorable, families were seen together for research purposes. These efforts continued into the early sixties, as clinicians recognized the ineffectiveness of traditional approaches with schizophrenia and delinquency. Family therapy, like psychoanalysis before it, began as a creative effort to find new solutions to old problems, even if the new ideas violated the conventional wisdom and common sense of the day.

The beginnings of family therapy represented a movement away from intrapsychic dynamics, which Freud had brought to the world's attention one-half century before, in favor of dyadic or two-person relationships. At first the mother-child relationship commanded the center of attention, with disturbances in this relationship considered causal to much of delinquent and schizophrenic behavior.

Later on the focus shifted. The family as a unit became the key to understanding and treating delinquency, schizophrenia, and most forms of emotional disorders. The interrelatedness of all family members, not just the mother-child interaction, emerged as the leitmotif of family therapy. If we include in this scheme the influence of at least three generations, we would be correct in saying that it still is today.

In family therapy the family came to be known as a system, an organized whole whose totality is more than just the sum of its parts or members. Clinical experience taught us to understand a family in the following way: as having rules, explicit and covert, consistent and contradictory, that regulate the behavior of its members; as having a tendency to maintain the status quo, but in healthy families also allowing for change and development; as having a structure that organizes the way members relate to one another and to the outside world; and as binding its members by a sense of loyalty and covert expectations.

Key Issues in Families

The Family as a System

In birth and death, in marriage and divorce, through childhood, adolescence, adulthood, and old age, in raising children and saying good-bye to them, in building a home and pursuing a career, in achievements and failures, the lives of family members impinge on each other. It has been said that the family is the primary and usually the most powerful emotional system to which individuals ever belong, a system that shapes and influences the course and outcome of all our lives (Carter and Orfanidis, 1976, p. 196). Family members are interdependent; the important decisions that I make affect my wife and child, the people whose lives are intertwined with mine, just as their actions affect me.

Changes in one part of the family prompt compensatory changes in the rest of the family. When all of the children in a family have grown up and left home, the parents are faced with adjusting to these new circumstances. If the mother has always stayed home with her children, she is then confronted with a home empty of children. She may decide to go to work or school, and she will have more time to spend with her husband. These changes affect him as well. Presented with the opportunity for increased intimacy with his wife, he may be called upon to make changes in his life: to stay home more and to plan more activities that include the two of them.

In pathological families the problems of one member can paradoxically hold the family together. In these families the so-called well members function at the expense of the "sick" member. They surreptitiously collude with the symptomatic member, usually labeled "mad" or "bad," to remain that way — for their sakes. An alienated family, for example, can become united in their efforts to expel or rescue a "sick" child. Without having a cause around which to unite, family members would be forced to face the fundamental isolation and false unity of their system.

Relationships tend to be reciprocal in a system. A nagging mother complements a hesitant child. A rescuer needs someone to rescue. Peacemakers need people to wage war. A villain requires an accuser. A saint contrasts with a sinner. A mother or father who is overly involved with a child needs the other parent to be distant and stay away, just as the distant parent relies on an enmeshed one to take up his or her unmet responsibilities. Thinking in terms of systems, blame does not fall completely on any one family member. Instead, a mutual working together and active participation of both sides make the relationship what it is.

Whenever a husband criticizes his wife's figure, for example, she accuses him of being a negligent father. With this he becomes enraged and threatens her. She screams that he is a coward, and he begins to hit her. At any time the vicious cycle could be halted by either party, but each time it continues uninterrupted, the scenario is the same: an escalating pattern of criticizing and blaming that terminates in violence.

Jay Haley (1963, p. 160), a pioneer family therapist, described the family as a system in another way. Living intimately with each other over a long period of time, family members set limits on what they will tolerate from one another. When one member exceeds a prescribed limit, others act to enforce it. These limit-setting responses define the rules of behavior for the family. In this way a family is a system with its own built-in self-governing process. Each member acts as a governor of the others so that the system is maintained and the status quo preserved.

A family is a self-correcting system, similar to the thermostatic system that heats a house. In one sense, the thermostat governs the system, since it controls the heat from the furnace and therefore the room temperature. In another sense, all components in the system are part of the governing process. The furnace responds to a signal from the thermostat. The thermostat responds to the room temperature, which responds to the heat from the furnace. No one element alone is responsible for the room temperature. To change the room temperature, simply opening the window — changing one element in the system — will not work. The cold air from outside lowers the room temperature, but then the lowered reading on the thermostat sets off the furnace, which burns fiercely to restore the room temperature. The only sure way to make a change in the system is to alter at least two elements simultaneously.

There is an important difference, however, between a thermostat and a family system. The ultimate governor of a household thermostat is an outsider, who fixes the temperature setting around which the system fluctuates. In a family no outsider sets the limits for family behavior: the limits are set by each member as he or she responds to the others. Family members struggle, then, not only to correct any deviant member, but also to become the one who makes the rules in the first place.

In fact, the rules develop over generations. These rules can be explicit — "Marry only someone of your own religion." Or they can be implicit — "Don't trust outsiders." Rules such as these fix the limits of acceptable behavior for the family. They can be broken or changed, but the process is usually slow and difficult. True, some members successfully break old family rules, but others put aside the rules momentarily only to discover later that they have turned to them again. Vowing never to be critical like his father, for example, a man might find that he has grown up to become a fault-finding parent himself.

Regarding systems, Murray Bowen (1978) speaks of triangles, the basic building blocks of relationships. Let us say tension exists between a husband and wife. The fact of the tension, if it becomes public, threatens the marital relationship. It is more perilous for the spouses to acknowledge their differences, which might seriously disrupt their relationship, than it is painful to continue as they are. Something happens to the tension, however. One or both parents divert it onto a child. The child then becomes the cause or scapegoat for family problems, and therefore the rallying point for the parents, who can at least agree that their child has problems. Or the child becomes a surrogate spouse and confidant for one parent while the other parent withdraws emotionally.

Accepting the role of scapegoat, or confidant, the child complies, out of loyalty to the family, from anxiety, or as a submission to the superior position of his or her parents. Such a role for a child is demoralizing and symptom-producing. But to understand these symptoms, one would have to recognize the part the marital relationship played in the development of these problems. The symptoms of the child — and they could be varied — are not explainable (or treatable) divorced from insights into the larger and more complex family system.

In short, tension between two people (parents) is directed onto a third person (child). The child then becomes symptomatic, while the parents' marital relationship remains intact, although tenuous and potentially conflictual. No one member and no single relationship can be fully comprehended apart from the other members and relationships.

In every family there arise issues of togetherness and separateness, of dependence and conformity to the family, and of independence and being different. Too much togetherness leads to emotional stuck-togetherness, from which a conflict emerges between personal goals and family unity. Various solutions are possible (Bowen, 1976). In the healthiest one, a balance is struck between autonomy and loyalty to the family; differences are not disqualified, but are tolerated and encouraged as a first step toward dialogue.

Fusion is another "solution." In fused or enmeshed relatedness, a person thinks, acts, and feels based on what the family rules and relationships mandate. Life becomes a pursuit of winning approval, seeking revenge for perceived rejection, or maneuvering others into the types of relationships in which one feels safe and comfortable. Self-identity is solely an outgrowth of family tradition, which dictates acceptable behavior. People trip over each other emotionally. Because it threatens togetherness, privacy is prohibited. Conflict and disharmony have to be hidden lest genuine differences emerge. Fusion, it should be kept in mind, is not all or nothing but exists on a continuum from completely fused individuals to those whose fused relatedness occurs at certain times with certain people.

Opposite, but equally destructive, is the third solution, which Bowen calls "emotional distance." Because intimacy draws him or her into a fusion of personalities, a family member becomes cut off emotionally. Often family therapists encounter individuals who are emotionally cut off from their families but who repeat intense but short-lived emotional involvements with others, as if they crave closeness but seem to be allergic to it. While the previous solution idolizes togetherness, this one canonizes distance.

Understanding a family as a system helps us to realize the profound impact parents and children have on each other. What parents do during divorce can alter the course of their children's lives; children's reaction to divorce can ease their parents pressures or multiply their cares. Knowing that a family is a system helps us appreciate the force a custody or visitation dispute can have on every family member, and it calls us to examine and try to help alter the family interrelationships if we hope to resolve a custody or visitation controversy. As a naturally occurring system, the family supports, controls, nurtures, and socializes its members (Minuchin, 1974); it is the context in which unique personalities and individual identities are either encouraged and fostered or thwarted and frustrated.

Loyalty and Justice

Trust, as Erikson (1963) has described, is the cornerstone of human development. It is so profound that all the rest of one's life is colored by its hue. A family is more than just a system of patterned, reciprocal, repetitive relationships that organizes the lives of its members. Family relationships are intimate and intensely personal, and like all human relationships, have or lack a quality of being viable and trustworthy.

A capacity for commitment and trust makes up the essence of all human relationships. Clinicians and many other people know this explicitly, but all of us know it at least implicitly. Enduring human relationships are built upon a reciprocity of fairness between people and generations, a balance between what one has done for one's family and what the family has done in return, between what one has omitted with one's family and what it has failed to do for the individual.

Boszormenyi-Nagy and Spark (1973) call this relational

ethics. Each person carries around an internal scale of justice, a ledger; etched on each ledger is the sense of whether or not the individual has been treated fairly in life and been found to be significant and important to others, especially one's family. On the ledger are written accounts of past and present obligations among family members and whether these obligations have been met or are in arrears. Taking their ideas and terminology from Martin Buber, a profound philosophical and religious twentieth-century thinker, Boszormenyi-Nagy and Spark have suggested that a person can have "a sense of injured justice," a feeling of being exploited or unfairly treated. Individuals who feel exploited go through their lives crusading for personal justice, always quick to take offense, angry, often demanding that others make up for what they missed.

Parent-child relationships are particularly vulnerable to exploitation. The intrinsic dependence of children on their parents makes them highly sensitive and susceptible to grievous mistakes, failures, or omissions by their parents. Parents, in turn, invest themselves in their offspring and may depend on their children's achievements to give them the primary joy and satisfaction that they find in life.

There is more to it than this, however. Basic to family relationships is a pervasive although often hidden sense of loyalty. Parents and children are obligated to each other, not as casual acquaintances but as people forever joined together by blood ties. They are intimately linked by family custom and history. A commitment to maintaining the family, to living up to family expectations, and to treating other family members in prescribed ways constitute the loyalty commitment intrinsic in each family. I often say to parents who are battling each other over custody or visitation that they are divorcing *each other*, not their children. Expressed in another context, I have frequently heard one spouse say to another: "*I* can criticize my parents, but don't *you* do it!" Loyalty ties among family members can be denied, hidden, invisible, minimized, or even exaggerated, but in a sense these ties can never be completely dissolved.

Loyalty and justice are core issues in family relationships and must be incorporated into any solution of a custody or visitation dispute. A custody or visitation settlement that violates children's natural loyalties to their parents, or one that injures any family member's sense of justice fails to achieve its purpose and only furthers the problems of the children and parents.

Justice is the bell that reverberates throughout a family's interactions. Boszormenyi-Nagy and Spark (1973) quote Dickens: "In the little world in which children have their existence, whosoever brings them up, there is nothing so finely perceived and so finely felt as injustice" (p. 65). Their second quote is from Piaget: "Reciprocity stands so high in the eyes of the child that he will apply it even where to us it seems to border on crude vengeance" (p. 65).

Justice excludes exploitation, which in regard to children can come in many forms. Thinking about and acting toward one's child as if he or she were a parent is a special form of exploitation, termed "parentification" (Boszormenyi-Nagy and Spark, 1973). It means making someone unfairly responsible for someone else. Although children need to identify with their parents and model some parental behavior as a preparation for adulthood, parentification goes far beyond this; it is the giving of excessive responsibility to a child, which interferes with a child's personal development.

Boszormenyi-Nagy and Spark have identified three kinds of parentification — emotional, sexual, aggressive — and I have added a fourth, functional, a sub-category of the first. In emotional parentification, parents overly depend on their children for emotional support, as if they need their children to survive psychologically. Children are expected to satisfy their parents' emotional needs; a parent derives self-esteem from his or her child's achievements but becomes depressed if the child fails. In this form of parentification, as in all forms, parent-child roles are reversed: Parents expect their children to make decisions for them, as if the children were really the parents and the parents, children. Incest and sexual molestation by parents comprise the second kind. Breaking the incest taboo and blurring the boundaries between generations, the parent treats a child as a sexual peer or partner. In cases of child abuse, when children become targets of parental rage and frustration, we have the third form. Abusing parents hold their children accountable for their frustration, expecting high levels of performance from them. If children fail to reach these heights, the parents become enraged, as if they have been personally deprived. Finally, when children are given excessive responsibilities at home — babysitting, raising younger children, running a household — responsibilities that interfere with their personal development as children, and which are done without parental guidance, there occurs functional parentification. (Boszormenyi-Nagy and Spark, 1973, talk about these activities in terms of parentification, but I feel they warrant a separate category.)

In all cases of parentification, a child is burdened with responsibility and prevented from being a child. A client of mine expressed this well when she said, "I was born a grown-up." She meant that she felt as if she always had adult responsibilities when she should have been attending school, socializing with her peers, dating, and maturing emotionally at her own pace.

Whatever injures a child's sense of justice and distorts the natural unfolding of loyalty between the generations exploits that child. Exploitation can also be situational or unavoidable. The death of a parent when a child is very young, especially if by that death the family is deeply disrupted and falls victim to hard times, is an unavoidably exploitative situation. Custody or visitation disputes are exploitative if through them a child's needs are ignored. In most cases, however, this is avoidable.

Exploitation can also occur under the guise of being permissive and tolerant. Instead of giving a child freedom from unnecessary constraint, permissiveness actually takes away from a child what is needed for growing up—limits, direction, guidance, and a definition of parental values. Since children are naturally obligated to give back to their parents something in return for all that they have received, the nonacceptance of repayment—often seen in parents who martyr themselves for their children—keeps a child forever obligated, never free to grow emotionally independent. It is therefore exploitative.

Children need constructive ways to express their loyalties to their parents. This can be done through achieving worthwhile goals, through active ways of showing affection such as writing letters or calling, through loving service to parents, especially when parents have grown old, or through mature emotional availability to parents.

In pathological families, a child's personal failure can be a way to demonstrate love or repay obligations; parents can worry about their children's failures at school, ruined marriages, loss of friends, or depression as a way of avoiding facing the pain and failure in their own lives or their marital disappointment. By failing to graduate college, an adult daughter, for example, protects her intelligent but uneducated mother from facing her—the mother's—lack of school accomplishment and the depression that she feels about it. Boszormenyi-Nagy and Spark term this negative loyalty: loyalty to the family that is destructive to the individual.

Parents and children are accountable to each other. Boszormenyi-Nagy and Spark (1973, pp. 88–89) have written that parents are accountable to raise their children to maturity, to set limits, and to demonstrate love, without either permissiveness or an arbitrary exercise of authority. It is irresponsible for parents to give little or nothing emotionally to their children, but it is just as irresponsible for parents not to expect and accept in return a fair consideration from their children for their efforts, for unless children can repay their parents emotionally they are forever indebted and never free to grow into independent adults. Children have a right to be raised responsibly by their parents; a right inherent in their position as children and one that does not have to be earned or merited. In essence then, a child needs and has a right to learn to develop a relationship with his or her parents that promotes trust and loyalty commitments based on mutual give-and-take and fairness.

The importance of give-and-take in human relationships should not be underestimated. Relationships that are one-sided, where one party always gives and the other always receives, lead to exploitation and injure each person's sense of justice. Children, therefore, are also accountable to their parents. They should be expected to make a meaningful contribution to their parents, family, and society, a contribution that is appropriate to their ages, personalities, and competence. But their needs should be met whether they succeed in contributing or fail in their efforts.

Balancing giving and receiving in relationships is not easy to do. Circumstances sometimes prohibit the unfolding of the responsibilities that parents and children have to each other. With serious personal problems or chronically unsatisfying marriages, some parents have great difficulties living up to their obligations. Peer pressure, cultural influences, and individual limitations can dissuade children from acting responsibly toward society, their families, and parents. Besides these are the tragic limitations of life, the fact of human error, ignorance, and prejudice, the reality of selfishness and self-centeredness, the unbridled and capricious exercise of power, the imperfectness of our world, the inadequate understanding we all have of ourselves, and the clash of values, of groups, and of ideologies. All of these limit and condition our accountability to each other, but they do not eradicate it.

SUMMARY

The reader who has gained a general understanding of the family therapy movement will appreciate that custody and visitation problems represent one form of family relationship problems. As unresolved marital and family problems get channeled into custody contests, the transition that should take place in family relationships and in the lives of family members does not occur. With these unsettled problems and the clash of parents' and children's interests, custody conflicts frustrate children's needs, lay waste to their sense of justice, and subvert the natural loyalties intrinsic to family relationships. With whatever problems it has, however, the family does not exist in a vacuum; it is part of a culture and a society. It is a product of that culture and that society, and in turn helps to create the culture and form the society. A grasp of each element — the individual, the family, the relational, and the cultural-legal — is necessary in order to achieve an understanding of what custody or visitation disputes are about and how to resolve them. The reader is advised to refer to this chapter throughout the book, since loyalty, justice, system, and other key concepts will be repeated often.

TWO

Historical Overview

CONCERN FOR THE RIGHTS of children evolved over time (Derdeyn, 1976). Roman law did not recognize such rights, but instead gave fathers unchallenged control over their children; fathers could with impunity condemn their children to death.

Essentially unchanged until the fourteenth century, this concept of absolute right persisted into English common law. In the Middle Ages childhood was not considered a specific developmental stage in life, as it is today. Children as young as seven were sent into apprenticeship, where the labor they performed for their masters was more important than what they learned. In the sixteenth century children began to have specific childhood tasks to master and to be considered as deserving of affection.

In eighteenth-century England, an almost absolute right to custody belonged to fathers. Since a father owned and managed all of the family property and had control over income and financial matters, it was considered unfeasible to remove a child from a father's custody lest the financial support of a child be jeopardized. English common law pronounced a father guardian of his children. Prior to the nineteenth century, custody of a child was essentially a property right of the natural parents, with fathers highly favored over mothers. The interests of the children, regardless of their ages, were not usually considered.

21

Gradually, however, custody came to mean obligations for parents, not just the fulfillment of a natural, unchallengeable prerogative. In the early part of the nineteenth century, English courts assumed jurisdiction over the welfare of children under the principle of *parens patriae*. This doctrine held that the Crown should protect all those who have no other protection. With this statute in mind, the Talfourd's Act of 1839 gave the courts power to determine custody of children under the age of seven.

Also in the nineteenth century, English law began to deviate from previous practice in cases where the father's behavior infuriated the court. Percy Bysshe Shelley, the poet, and his wife were involved in a custody dispute (Shelley v. Westbrooke). Shelley was refused custody because of his "vicious and immoral" atheistic beliefs. As judicial attitudes changed, the rule evolved that mothers generally should get custody of daughters and fathers of sons, unless the children were very young. Helping to shape this change in England was the Guardianship of Infants Act of 1925, under which the right of mothers to custody was gradually increased. For a short time in both the United States and England, the law proclaimed the equality of mothers and fathers with respect to custody of their children.

In the United States, a superior right to custody generally accrued to fathers until the twentieth century. This was based on a long tradition in English common law, buttressed by the practical consideration of a father's financial advantage, which in effect made children the property of their fathers. So much did financial capabilities underlie a father's claim to custody that a father deprived of custody could be excused from his financial obligations to his child. Not until the early 1900s did the idea develop that a father has some responsibility to his children whether or not he has received custody. Now the way was cleared for mothers to be considered seriously for custody. Other developments, however, were taking place that eventually placed women in the forefront of obtaining custody of their children.

As industrialization emerged in the eighteenth and nineteenth centuries, men went out of their homes to work. The care and feeding of children was left to mothers, who came to do most of the child-rearing. Just as fathers had been favored in custody matters because of a historical situation — superior financial status — the preeminent claim to custody that evolved for mothers was rooted in a social reality — namely, their staying home to care for their children. Laws and customs became a justification for the status quo, and as mothers gained in their ability to obtain custody, laws and social attitudes solidified. It has been said (Roman and Haddad, 1978) that a mother's superior claim to custody disenfranchised her rather than enhancing her position in society. It can still be argued that maternal custody entails greater confinement to the home and therefore keeps women out of the labor force.

There were other influential trends leading to maternal custody. The status of women in society was rising. They secured the right to vote, the ability to own property, and increased employment opportunities. These all augmented the developing rights of women with respect to custody. The notion that fathers had an obligation to pay child support even if they did not obtain custody had cleared away a primary obstacle to mothers receiving custody.

Attitudinal changes also occurred, which, in short, can be expressed by the idea of the maternal presumption. This means that a mother's claim to custody, which grew out of social necessity and circumstances, developed into a presumption which then became entrenched in American judicial and cultural attitudes.

Underlying this shift in custody practices was another notion — the "tender years" presumption. The mother's right to custody emerged slowly; it started out as her right to obtain custody of young children. In the early 1900s an increased interest in early childhood development turned attention to the needs of infants and young children. The result was that maternal care came to be considered necessary for very young children. The courts were beginning to award custody to mothers anyway, and the tender years presumption increased this tendency. By the twentieth century the first traces of the "best interests of the child" criterion can be seen. Instead of becoming a standard for deciding custody by asserting as primary the rights and needs of children, it did more at first to ensure the advantage mothers were gaining in custody decisions (Derdeyn, 1976).

Along with the assertion of a mother's claim to custody, the advantage of fathers waned. As we know, throughout most of the middle third of this century, mothers have acquired a superior claim to custody.

PRESENT TRENDS

Child custody practices are evolving again. Shifts are evident in social attitudes toward child-rearing and the roles and responsibilities of fathers and mothers. As the status of women continues to change, they more frequently assert their rights to equality of opportunity in the marketplace and parity with men in social relations. Some mothers prefer not to seek custody. Fathers are no longer content to be only part-time or weekend parents or to be considered peripheral to child-rearing. More fathers are seeking and gaining custody, although mothers are still favored in practice. The rapid increase in the divorce rate and the number of single-parent families is altering the nature of family life in the United States: previously accepted assumptions about child custody, child-rearing, and the ideal of the two-parent family will require reexamination. Increased concern and understanding of childhood, prompted by the growth of developmental psychology—especially under the master strokes of Jean Piaget and Erik H. Erikson—and psychoanalytic thinking initiated by Freud, have helped us to appreciate that child-hood is a distinct stage in the life cycle, with specific tasks, challenges, and obstacles. As we understand children and childhood better, we should apply that understanding to child custody questions.

Recently, joint custody and coparenting have begun to command the attention of lawmakers, the judiciary, parents, and mental health professionals. Joint custody, a legal arrangement, means that parents share equally in the rights and responsibilities of child-rearing after divorce (Nehls and Morgenbesser, 1980). This does not necessarily include joint or shared living arrangements. Coparenting means that parents have agreed between themselves to cooperate as parents and to share in the decision making of child-rearing.

As evidence of the changing trends in child custody decisions — and perhaps as a result of it — the maternal presumption and the tender years doctrine are losing influence. As of 1978, twenty-three states have passed legislation explicitly stipulating that the sex of a parent should not be a factor in determining custody (Hebb, 1978). The American Psychological Association Council of Representatives at their January 1977 meeting approved the following resolution (cited in Salk, 1977):

> Be it resolved that the Council of Representatives recognizes officially and makes suitable promulgation of the fact that it is scientifically and psychologically baseless, as well as in violation of human rights, to discriminate against men because of their sex in assignment of children's custody, in adoption, in the staffing of child-care services, in personnel practices providing for parental leave in relation to childbirth and emergencies involving children, and in similar laws and practices. [P. 50]

In discussing the idea that mothers are presumed to be better able to serve the needs of children, Dr. Lee Salk (1977) argues the following: it deprives a child of constitutional rights to due process of law; the issues of custody and visitation are decided before they are heard. Based on cultural presumptions and prejudices, it is unscientific. It may also be harmful to a child, because a father in fact may be better suited for custody, and it may alienate a father from his child by encouraging him not to be closely involved.

In preparing a report for the Maine Civil Liberties Union in July 1978 regarding child custody in Maine, Dorcas Hebb (1978) concluded that maternal presumption is weakening in her state. She reported that other data collected is conflicting, however, so she concluded that perhaps lawyers discourage fathers from seeking custody because they think maternal presumption is still the rule in Maine. The report cites a recent American Law Report which points out that the overall trend is that maternal presumption is no longer a rule that can only be overturned by compelling evidence. It is becoming a rule that is applicable only as a tie breaker when other factors are equal.

Two other present trends should be noted. According to Derdeyn (1976), there has been a slight decline in practice of using the norm of parental culpability in custody contests. In the last century, a parent who was found at fault for the divorce was not considered favorably in custody disputes. The interests of the child, it was thought, were better served if the parent not at fault was given custody. When the "fault" was adultery, the courts were even more likely to favor the other parent. While fault is sometimes an easy index for settling complex custody cases, it is not necessarily a justifiable one. Adultery per se is not likely to interfere with parenting. Also, we are now seeing a movement away from using fault as grounds for divorce.

The issue of sex discrimination between parents regarding custody decisions is also receiving attention. Derdeyn (1976) argues that to say that a young child is uniquely in need of maternal care constitutes differential treatment of the parents on the basis of sex, perhaps a problem in terms of the Fourteenth Amendment. The previous quote from the American Psychological Association Council of Representatives (pp. 42–43) makes the same point. There was a time when a mother had to be shown to be unfit for a father to be awarded custody. Now, even though a mother may be fit, a father can receive custody if he is judged better able to care for his child.

"Unwed Father Wins Child Custody, Sets New York State Precedent" was the headline of an article that appeared in the *Philadelphia Inquirer* (May 23, 1979, p. 7A). The news item reports that an Albany County Family Court awarded custody of a seven-month-old child to her twenty-three-year-old father. It was the first time in the state's history that a custody dispute involving unwed parents was resolved in the father's favor. The court's decision, which the mother was planning to appeal, was based on "the best interests of the child."

It should be kept in mind that these trends — the weakening of maternal presumption and the tender years doctrine, more fathers gaining custody, the lessening of sex discrimination, and marital fault declining as a relevant factor in custody decisions — are fairly new and their implementation in practice varies. Long-standing cultural assumptions, as with most entrenched belief systems or behavioral patterns, do not yield easily to new ways.

Best Interests of the Child

Along with the maternal presumption, the most important trend of the twentieth century regarding custody decisions is the "best-interests-of-the-child" criterion. In the early part of this century the criterion did more to strengthen a mother's access to custody than to provide a standard for awarding custody based on inherent needs of a child. Now more emphasis is being placed on the genuine interests of a child, which at least in theory is the preeminent principle for deciding custody.

In 1974 the American Bar Association approved the Uniform Marriage and Divorce Act (National Conference of Commissioners on Uniform State Laws, 1970), a model legislation that is having its impact in judicial circles. Regarding the best interests of the child, it reads:

> The court shall determine custody in accordance with the best interests of the child. The court shall consider all relevant factors including:
> (1) The wishes of the child's parent or parents as to his custody;
> (2) The wishes of the child as to his custody;
> (3) The interaction and interrelationship of the child and any other person who may significantly affect the child's best interest;
> (4) The mental and physical health of all individuals involved. [Sec. 402, p. 45]

Regarding visitation, the legislation reads:

> (a) A parent not granted custody of the child is entitled to reasonable visitation rights unless the court finds, after a hearing, that visitation would endanger the child's physical health or significantly impair his emotional development.
> (b) The court may modify an order granting or denying visitation rights whenever modification would serve the best interests of the child; but the court shall not restrict a parent's visitation rights unless it finds that the visitation would endanger the child's physical health or significantly impair his emotional development. [Sec. 407, p. 49]

Bernstein (1977) cites the 1975 Oregon divorce law as stating that preference in custody should not be given to the mother over the father simply because she is the mother. He noted a recent Florida Divorce Law that indicates that custody and visitation rights of minor children should be decided in accordance with the best interests of the child and that the father and mother should be given the same consideration in these decisions.

Lee Salk (1977) believes that it is highly destructive to ignore the best interests and wishes of the child regarding custody. He wrote that it leads to a syndrome characterized by "the feeling of helplessness, destructiveness, defiance, low motivation, acting out, as well as feelings of abandonment" (p. 50).

LEAST DETRIMENTAL ALTERNATIVE

An alternative to the best interests of the child criterion has been proposed. Goldstein, Freud, and Solnit, in their now famous work, *Beyond the Best Interests of the Child* (1973), recommend "the least detrimental alternative" as a new standard. They describe it in this way:

> The least detrimental alternative, then, is that specific placement and procedure for placement which maximizes, in accord with the child's sense of time and on the basis of short-term predictions given the limitations of knowledge, his or her opportunity for being wanted and for maintaining on a continuous basis a relationship with at least one adult who is or will become his psychological parent. [P. 53]

They go on to explain why a new guideline is suggested:

> Even though we agree with the manifest purpose of the "in-the-best-interests-of-the-child" standard, we adopt a new guideline for several reasons. First, the traditional standard does not, as the phrase "least detrimental," convey to the decisionmaker that the child in question is already a victim of his environmental circumstances, that he is greatly at risk, and that speedy action is necessary to avoid further harm being done to his chances of healthy psychological development. Secondly, the old guideline, in context and as construed by

legislature, administrative agency, and court, has come to mean something less than what is in the child's best interests. The child's interests are often balanced against and frequently made subordinate to adult interests and rights. Moreover, and less forthrightly, many decisions are "in-name-only" for the best interests of the specific child who is being placed. They are fashioned primarily to meet the needs and wishes of competing adult claimants or to protect the general policies of a child care or other administrative agency. But, even if the child's rights were, in fact and policy, determinative and thus unequivocally superior to adult interests, the guideline would remain inadequate. [P. 54]

These authors argue that a child is already a victim of a divorce and custody contest and is therefore at high risk. Speedy action by the court is necessary to avoid increasing the chances of psychological harm. Children need a continuous relationship with a loving adult. Such a relationship can be jeopardized by lengthy, bitter custody disputes. The authors suggest this new standard as a way of discouraging the decision makers from unrealistic hopes and from deluding themselves into thinking that they have a greater power for doing good than for doing harm.

The least detrimental alternative guideline is needed for another reason. The authors argue that the standard of the best interests of the child is only given lip service anyway; in practice, as the above quote indicates, adult interests prevail. The fallibility of any decision maker, furthermore, is made clearer by this standard. Another reason for this new standard is that the number of feasible options available for placement is limited anyway.

For several reasons I agree in part with the least detrimental alternative standard. The emotional vulnerability of children during a divorce is greatly increased by bitter, protracted custody or visitation conflicts. In my opinion, the greatest harm to a child occurs when his or her needs are set aside or ignored because of a parent's need for winning custody and defeating the other parent. Parents, moreover, may be so overwhelmed by a divorce as to be emotionally unavailable to their children. Worse, children can become tools in their parents' marital struggles, which do not necessarily end with divorce but continue to be played out in custody or visitation contests. The least detrimental alternative reminds us that custody battles run a high risk of exploiting children. It also reminds us that there are no ideal solutions to these problems; pain accompanies the disruption of any significant interpersonal relationship or profound changes in life-style.

Summary

Laws and attitudes toward custody have evolved; they were not always what they are today. Nor need they be tomorrow what they are now. Laws and customs are socially conditioned. For example, at one time a father's financial superiority and higher social status meant he had an almost unchallengeable right to custody. Then industrialization and the somewhat improved status of women helped to change the laws in favor of mothers.

As laws and practices change, they solidify and mold social attitudes. For instance, as laws came to favor them, mothers came to be presumed better suited for child-rearing. The mother's superior claim to custody, which dominated child custody practices for most of the twentieth century, grew out of a justification for the circumstances of the family and child-rearing in the last century. Later it was reinforced by the changed status of women in the early part of this century.

But a mother's superior claim to custody and the supposition that women are naturally better at child-rearing are presumptions. As such, they are unproven and unjustifiable; they are based upon another unverified assumption, namely, the tender years doctrine.

Although it has been given lip service for years, the best

interests of the child as a standard for deciding custody disputes is only now beginning to be addressed seriously. Custody is increasingly being granted based on what would be helpful, or least harmful, to children, not on presumptive parental rights, biases in favor of men or women, sex discrimination, or parental culpability in divorce. The shift in favor of children's best interests, however, is still more in theory than in practice.

There is now a great emphasis on childhood as a distinct developmental stage, with children seen as having specific tasks to master and inherent rights as human beings, not simply as children of their parents. More than before parents are considered to have corresponding obligations to their children. At one time, for example, fathers had no financial responsibilities unless they had custody.

Economic and social conditions are changing again: women press for greater independence and a lessening of their financial and social inequality with men; men assert their child-rearing capabilities; single parenthood is increasing. More often, judges think in terms of joint custody, and parents consider coparenting.

Judicial decisions and social attitudes regarding child custody ought to change again. Instead of just being given lip service, the interests of children should become in truth the ultimate criteria for custody decisions; social prejudice or presumption regarding either parent should not be used to decide custody.

THREE

Reactions of Children

LIFE IS NOT A SMOOTH unfolding of a pre-established plan; rather, it develops in stages characterized by crises, choices, and transitions (Erikson, 1963). It involves the themes of engagement and separation, of making commitments and of changing directions. Change is as much a part of life as is continuity. Separation or disengagement occurs throughtout the life cycle. The first day of school, the profound psychological changes of adolescence, marriage, death, children leaving home, are all examples. Divorce is also a separation. It is a transition where a specific life-style is overturned and an important interpersonal relationship lost or jeopardized, or at least drastically altered. For a divorcing parent, the changes in life-style are massive. Usually income is decreased. In most cases, one parent becomes the primary caretaker, another a weekly or monthly parent. The marital relationship ends at least legally. Whether or not this is a relief, it nevertheless marks a severe change in one's interpersonal world.

For a child, the changes concomitant with a divorce are even more weighty and stressful. A major change takes place in the child's relationship with the noncustodial parent as well as with the custodial one. Contact with that parent is lessened, minimized, or lost. Financial pressures may curtail former recreation and activities. Moving means new schools,

33

new friends, and new surroundings. Babysitters and surrogate caretakers increase. Some children are confronted with their parents' new girlfriends or boyfriends and perhaps their children. There may be a sense of relief at the cessation of overt conflict, but divorce prompts massive changes in a child's and family's life and is consequently extremely stressful.

REACTIONS TO DIVORCE OR SEPARATION

Children have various reactions to divorce, and individual children react differently. Reactions can be general and diffuse (loyalty conflicts), and over the long run they can interfere with personal development. Or they can be specific, as when the child develops emotional, physical, or behavioral symptoms such as denial, depression, regression, anger, guilt feelings, reconciliation preoccupations, anxiety, lowered self-esteem, and fears of abandonment.

Loyalty Conflicts

As I indicated in the first chapter, family members have natural ties and loyalties to each other. Although powerful, these loyalties can be invisible (Boszormenyi-Nagy and Spark, 1973), and they are often denied or minimized. Nevertheless they are a fundamental reality of family life. A loyalty conflict is particularly likely in a divorce and intense custody or visitation dispute, for a child finds it extremely difficult to maintain a sense of loyalty to parents who are at war with each other and who directly or indirectly disparage the other parent and discourage a child's positive feelings toward either parent. The most beneficial situation for a child is to have a positive psychological relationship with both parents, while each parent encourages the child's relationship to the other parent.

Loyalty conflicts come in many forms. Although a child wants in most cases to maintain positive ties to both parents, divided or split loyalty occurs when he or she is implicitly asked to take sides between battling parents. In this situation a child cannot be loyal to one parent without jeopardizing his or her relationship with the other parent. Adolescents who run back and forth between their divorced parents' homes are often motivated by divided loyalty. A child can secretly hold in admiration the absent parent, identifying with and acting like him or her, but be unable to express this openly and work it through for fear of offending the other parent. In a family I counseled the adolescent daughter, who lived with her father and stepmother, partly identified with her absent mother, who was irresponsible, violent, promiscuous, and alcoholic. At times this adolescent could be kind and well behaved, but thoughts of or actual contact with her mother triggered her acting out. She followed her father and stepmother's rules for conduct part of the time, but then, in loyalty to her mother, she followed her mother's behavioral patterns (even though her mother verbally discouraged her). I was unsuccessful in bringing these parents (mother, father, and stepmother) together with the daughter to work out a viable loyalty system in which the girl could identify with the positive aspects of both parents and have the green light from all of them to do this. The biological mother was too embittered at the girl's father to genuinely endorse a positive loyalty to him, and she gave the adolescent no constructive way to be loyal to her. The stepmother, threatened by the presence of the girl's mother, discouraged her husband from contact with her, contact that could have helped the girl avoid a loyalty conflict.

An unhealthy response to a loyalty conflict is manifested when a child forms a coalition with one parent against the other parent. Here a child violates usual loyalty definitions by choosing one parent and rejecting the other. Mostly this is done with the encouragement of the aligning parent. It is the child's attempt to gain the approval of at least one parent, approval that seemingly cannot be gotten in more constructive ways. The child is then likely to develop a distorted view of both parents, seeing one as ideal and the other as villainous. The child's identification process suffers, since it is impossible to live up to an ideal image and destructive to emulate a villainous one. A child may, for example, learn to side with women and distrust men, or vice versa.

Out of loyalty some children attempt to hold up their parents emotionally, while neglecting important developmental concerns of their own. Parents encourage this when they seek custody because they emotionally need their children. In the first chapter this was referred to as emotional parentification. Sensitive to the stress that accompanies the breakup of a family, a child can act "crazy" or "bad" as an attempt to hold his or her family together, even if it is by the thin thread of uniting everyone to help him or her. Children involved in bitter custody contests, especially adolescents, can be called upon to take responsibility for the family home and their younger siblings, and can end up making important family decisions in the absence of their parents. I call these children "functionally parentified."

In all instances of parentification, a child is given and accepts unfair responsibility for other family members, even parents; all of this is done at the expense of the child's personal development and opportunities for growth. Little time or energy is available to be a child or adolescent. Legitimate childhood or adolescent pursuits are put aside so that the family's needs can be addressed.

Loyalty conflicts result in diverse behavioral problems. A child fails school and consequently distracts his or her parents from their marital distress. An adolescent attempts suicide so that his workaholic father is drawn more directly into the family living. A woman is unable to enjoy sex with her husband. Throughout her life her mother confided in her about how she felt humiliated by her husband's sexual demands.

Siding with her mother, the woman learned to hate her father and believes that all men exploit women.

Loyalty conflicts can also become manifested in diffuse personal problems. A married daughter feels she has no life of her own. She also neglects her husband and children because she is always available to her mother. She frequently runs errands for her mother and calls her daily to listen to her inveigh about the mother's own mother who lives next door. These services take important time away from the daughter's marriage, which suffers, and stops her from enjoying leisure time with her friends. A man is chronically depressed due to constant worry about his aged parents, who fight with each other and neglect their health. He believes he should make them happy, but can't.

A child also has specific reactions to divorce. These reactions are viewed through the lens of intrapsychic dynamics.* Children may have one or several of the following reactions.

Denial

As the most basic defense humans have against facing painful situations, denial is universal. So distressing is a separation from one parent that a child denies it has taken place. Denial shows itself in various permutations. For example, a child makes up excuses for the noncustodial parent's absence. Whenever that parent calls or comes to the house, the child assumes that the parent will stay for an extended time. A child may disavow concern about the separation, but instead manifest excessive preoccupation with another person or pet. Idealizing the absent parent, the child insists that he or she is loving and concerned despite the parent's not visiting or not providing financial support.

---

*Much of the material regarding individual reactions is based on Richard A. Gardner's book *Psychotherapy with Children of Divorce.* New York: Jason Aronson, 1976.

Parents encourage denial when they hide their differences and conflicts so that their children cannot see that all human relationships involve struggle. In some families the rule is that problems or painful issues should be avoided, lest someone be offended. When a separation occurs, the only way it can be dealt with in such families is for the child to deny it has actually happened.

By not openly communicating feelings, parents encourage their children to do the same. Parents may reason that a child is too young or sensitive to witness marital discord, yet often it is the parents themselves who are too anxious and threatened to admit to the conflict. They attribute these feelings to the children, who are then mystified or confused because the parents are defining their experience and feelings for them. This is an example of what Laing (1972) calls a transpersonal defense, an attempt by one person to control the thoughts and feelings of another in order to protect the first person's own psychic stability. Denial — and regression, which will be discussed later — are intrapsychic defenses that a person builds in himself or herself in order to avoid anxiety or threats to safety, security, or self-esteem. Transpersonal defenses are done to another person for the sake of the first individual. These defenses are most common between parents and children. Being the stronger person emotionally, a parent can impose certain experiences on a child who has little choice but to accept the world as defined by the parent. Rather than this, children need to experience the world for themselves under their parents' guidance, to gradually learn to think, act, and feel for themselves, and not to have someone else impose his or her version of the world on them.

A parent may act as if the other, absent parent does not exist and prohibit the children from talking about that parent or about the separation. Parents encourage denial if they discourage an open, appropriate expression of feelings. Parents should keep in mind that children are subject to the family conflicts whether or not the conflicts are discussed in front of them.

Anger

A child can become angry when he or she can no longer deny the fact of a divorce. Anger results from frustration of needs and goals or from the sense of being unfairly treated or exploited (injured justice). Gardner lists several reasons for a child's anger. Marital discord deprives a child of a loving environment. A child easily feels abandoned. Parents sometimes scapegoat their children, blaming them for their own unhappiness. Perhaps a child reminds a parent of the other hated spouse. The custodial parent may have to work and therefore is absent from home more. Either parent can resent a child who is seen as a burden or a restriction of the parent's freedom. The child may feel different from other children who have two parents. I would add that a child may feel angry if he or she has been asked to shoulder excessive responsibilities within the family, whether these are chores or emotional dependence by either parent. A parent who faces pervasive life-style changes may, willingly or inadvertently, neglect a child. Anger results if a child wanted his or her separated parents to stay together. Having to move, changing schools and friends, or suffering a diminishment of recreation due to financial strain can also provoke frustration and anger.

A child may be disallowed from expressing angry feelings openly or may lack constructive ways to cope with them. Then anger is denied or expressed in other forms, such as nightmares or temper tantrums. Repressed anger can turn up as tension or anxiety attacks. Anger is sometimes one of the dynamics behind phobias, compulsions, or depression.

Anger can be acted out as a way of calling attention to the child's and family's plight, as a signal to outside authorities or friends that help is needed, or as a direct expression of hostility. Anger is approved of by parents when they encourage a child to act out their own hostilities so that the parents can deny their own feelings. In particularly destructive cases, a child may be given a mission by one parent to act out against or hate the other parent, or to embody and express unacceptable parts of one parent's personality (Stierlin, 1977). The child's emotional development can be neglected so that in certain areas of functioning direct expression of anger is inappropriately encouraged. The child who identifies with parental hostility, revenge, power struggles, or violence may also act out. Acting out of anger is also a way to gain some recognition from either parent; it is better to have a punishing parent who at least recognizes the existence of a child than an indifferent one. Acting out may provoke a spurious sense of power, which is an attempt to offset feelings of impotence and helplessness. Acting out can express devotion to the family; parents who have to cope with a troublesome youth temporarily forget their own pain. Needing reassurance that the custodial parent won't leave too, a child acts out to test the parent's tolerance and commitment. Acting out sometimes avoids intimacy — reject the parent before he or she rejects you. Finally, acting out can be a direct expression of revenge by the child against a parent.

Depression

As a child recognizes that the divorce is a fact and the separation from one parent will last or at least the relationship will be significantly altered, anger yields to depression. Gardner reminds us that a child of divorce has something to be depressed about. A relationship with at least one parent is disrupted, perhaps lost, and the loss of a significant human relationship can be a devastating experience for anyone. The child's world changes drastically, resulting in the loss of previous enjoyments or activities. Angry and unable to express openly these feelings or act them out, a child turns them inward; depression ensues. Depression is also a reaction if a child perceives the separation as a personal rejection.

A parent would do well to scrutinize his or her child for signs of depression: loss of appetite, diminished concentration, loss of interest in school, apathy, withdrawal from friends, loss of enjoyment, direct expressions of despair or hopelessness, chronic irritability, self-depreciation, or threats of suicide. I counseled a child who threatened suicide as an attempt to bring his estranged father back to the family. In a family counseling session I learned that only when one of the children was ill did the father come to the home or pay attention to any of the children. This boy was able to acknowledge that he felt that if he was seriously ill — suicide threats would be a symptom — then his father would surely return to the family.

Brief periods and temporary manifestations of the above symptoms are normal, but lasting or intense symptoms augur more serious problems. Grief, furthermore, should be distinguished from depression. Like an adult, a child needs time to adjust to a separation. Sadness or grief reactions to divorce are usual, probably necessary. Helping a child work through grief can be a great service by a parent. During this time a child can be preoccupied with the absent parent, questioning the custodial parent repeatedly about him or her. The child needs explicit approval to express feelings about the divorce, even feelings that the parent finds painful, and to be allowed to ask questions, so that a gradual desensitization to the loss can take place. This working through of the separation is facilitated by regular and meaningful contact with the non-custodial parent and by the explicit approval of both parents for a child to maintain or initiate positive contact and feelings with either parent. As a child faces his or her sadness and pain with the parents' encouragement, adjustment and a restoration of self-esteem takes place.

Regression

If the custody or visitation dispute is lengthy and bitter, the divorce or separation can be so stressful to the child as to impair further psychological development or spark a regression to less mature behavioral patterns. Family relationships, particularly parent-child ones, often reinforce regression or impairment. Since custody and visitation disputes are usually continuations of previous marital and family problems, the forces within the family that lead to post divorce impairment may have already been present. The stress of a divorce and custody contest exacerbates the pathological family relationships, and these trigger the child's regression.

Signs of regression or impediments to further development include excessive demands or clinging by the child, the loss of previously attained skills such as toilet training, the disruption of a child's relationship with peers, school phobia, and interference with sleeping or eating patterns. All of these reflect the stress of a divorce and the upheaval of an involved custody dispute. Provided they are transitory, these reactions are normal. Chronic or intense reactions indicate serious problems.

Since the perspective of this book is the inevitable interlocking of individual needs and traits with family relationship patterns, it is important to note that regression is not only an individual child being overwhelmed by stress. Equally important, it is also a product of disturbances in the family relationships.

Parents can encourage regression by overindulgence and overinvolvement, both of which hide the parents' real dependency on their children. Overindulgence promotes incompetence instead of emotional maturity and developmental skills. A child who refuses to attend school is subtly rewarded for staying home, because in being at home the child keeps his or her lonely parent company. A parent's loneliness is assuaged and the child feels important. Parents can become so involved with their children that if one of them receives a rebuke from a peer or teacher, the parent takes it as a personal affront. Continually doing for children what they can do for themselves is overinvolvement. Some parents speak for their children, as if they know how their children feel or what they think before their children speak. Regression is encouraged when a parent refuses to listen or take the child seriously, thus discouraging a child's ability to test reality. The parent argues that the child is not angry or depressed, feelings that are too threatening for the parent to acknowledge. The child is just upset or annoyed.

Besides hidden dependency on a child, parents foster regression because of their guilt feelings. Parents who feel they have failed their children because of the breakup of the family, the absence of the noncustodial parent, or for the real or imagined neglect of a child while they are struggling to cope with the separation attempt to lessen their guilt through overindulgence. A child is not properly disciplined for fear the child will dislike his or her parent. A child is not expected to perform any household chores lest he or she be inconvenienced.

As an attempt to win a child's allegiance or to have a child form a coalition with one parent against the other one, a parent may overly gratify his or her child. Then the child is used as a replacement for the absent parent. Parents who feel they emotionally owe and are indebted to their own parents, without the hope of repayment, can overindulge their children as if they were the parent's parents. With this in mind, family therapy has helped us to recognize that marital and family problems cannot be treated separately from the parents' relationship with their own parents. A multigenerational perspective is essential.

Because a child is vulnerable during a divorce and custody battle, there is a greater need for attention and emotional support. It is hoped that all parents derive satisfaction and emotional rewards from raising their children. But serious harm results when attention becomes overindulgence and satisfaction becomes parentification and places the burden of excessive responsibilities on a child. Excessive gratification is not giving at all; in fact, it is taking away appropriate limits and self-constraint. Even more crippling is the indulgence of a child done as the parent's primary method of gaining self-esteem and emotional security. Exploited and victimized, a child is likely to experience anger, rage, and a sense of injured justice.

In reaction to divorce and particularly to an intense custody contest, children may not only regress; some also learn to overfunction or be hypermature. The maturity, however, is bogus. A child assumes parental roles and responsibilities, for example, to take care of the younger children without parental supervision.

Lowered Self-Esteem

Self-esteem is the foundation upon which much of subsequent emotional development is based; its absence is responsible for considerable inner conflict and turmoil throughout an individual's life. Self-esteem begins in childhood. A divorce and custody conflict can cut deeply into a child's resources. The loss of a parent or the absence or interference of a stable psychological relationship with a loving adult leads to feelings of worthlessness, incompetence, and low self-esteem.

Low self-esteem is associated with feeling abandoned and rejected. A child needs to feel important and significant to at least one adult. At first self-worth is measured by the extent to which a child feels valued by his or her parents or parent. A child can interpret divorce as a personal rejection, not as a marital conflict between adults. If the family life is typified by chronic and bitter conflict, especially if the conflict is blamed on the child, a child's self-esteem suffers. The fact of the separation and breakup of the family means instability in the child's world, in the face of which he or she feels uncertain and vulnerable, not knowing whether or not it can happen again.

Loyalty conflicts impinge on a child's self-esteem, since a child who feels it is disloyal to identify with either parent is robbed of an important aspect of development. Similarly, a child who idealizes one parent and scapegoats the other is subject to the same dangers.

A child who is seen as a burden to the custodial parent who has substantial adjustments to make comes to feel exploited and unloved. A noncustodial parent who becomes emotionally absent from his or her child conveys the message that the child is not important enough to be involved with. Since no child can be a parent to either of his or her parents, parentified children are inevitably exploited and likely to experience feelings of worthlessness.

Fears of Abandonment

Fears of abandonment, according to Gardner (1976), can refer to unwarranted fears. Although the custodial parent is committed and responsible to the child, the child may still fear that the parent will leave. Perhaps the child already feels abandoned by the parent who left. The child reasons that the same thing will happen again.

These unwarranted fears of abandonment should lessen in time as a child learns they are unfounded. A positive relationship with both parents encourages such a resolution. The child needs to be reassured that he or she will be cared for, even if the custodial parent dies. The breakup of the marriage, a child should learn, was on account of marital conflicts, not the child.

Fears of being abandoned can be justified because some children are truly neglected. Preoccupied with personal problems, massive life-style changes, financial pressures, social isolation, new surroundings and relationships, guilt feelings, unresolved emotional attachment to the former mate, anger, and depression, a parent may have few emotional resources left over for child-rearing. Worse, parents can be so intent upon securing revenge against each other or in proving their competence as parents at the expense of one another that they neglect the needs of their children.

The parents' relationship with each other can be so conflictual that the custodial parent tries to prevent visitation by the other parent. In the same sense, the absent parent may be so angry at the custodial parent that he or she attempts to get revenge by emotional and financial neglect of the child. Some custodial parents scapegoat the other parent in an attempt to shore up the fragile unity of the remaining family, but only a false unity and security is gained by setting themselves against the noncustodial parent, who is regarded as the enemy.

In my approach to custody and visitation problems, I try to engage the absent parent in therapy. This intervention is directed toward lessening the animosities between the parents enough to allow them to be parents. If this is impossible, I try to help the custodial parent explain to his or her child why the other parent is uninvolved, while carefully avoiding a scapegoating of that parent. I encourage the custodial parent to demonstrate to the child how he or she has sincerely tried to encourage positive contact with the other parent, thus trying to preserve the child's trust in at least one parent.

A child who experiences separation anxiety may not want to go to school or may protest when the parent goes to work. Excessive clinging may take place. Often, this is as much the parent's problem as the child's. The child fears abandonment and is afraid to leave the parent for school, but the parent in these cases usually depends on the child and encourages a lack of individuation. The child's clinging reinforces the parent's sense of being needed and important: the parent needs to be needed.

On account of fears of abandonment, a child provokes his or her parents. To a child, punishment is an assurance that the parents are still involved, at least to some extent.

Guilt

Guilt is an unpopular topic today. I attribute this to two reasons. One is that people have a built-in taboo against exploring personal failures of genuine responsibilities; it is always easy to blame the other and excuse the self. A second reason derives from a confusion between existential guilt and neurotic guilt feelings.

Martin Buber (1965) delineated the notion of existential guilt. The guilt that encumbers a person as a result of injuring another human being he calls existential guilt. Parents who fail repeatedly to meet their children's needs or who use their children mostly for their own ends, treating them as excessive baggage or chattel, incur existential guilt. They have offended their personal relationships with their children in a way commonly recognized as exploitative. Existential guilt does not depend on *feeling* guilty; it is matter of *being* guilty.

Existential guilt or the possibility of it is inherent in all human relationships, and it is especially applicable to parent-child interaction, since parents have intrinsic responsibilities to their children and children have certain obligations to parents. Chronic failure in these responsibilities tears apart the fabric of human existence and the loyalties between generations. Because these responsibilities can be neglected, there is the possibility of existential guilt. Because no parent or child is perfect, there is the fact of existential guilt. Existential guilt, then, is the reality of failing in one's genuine obligations or responsibilities.

Neurotic guilt feelings, on the other hand, are incapacitating feelings of worthlessness and self-depreciation which do nothing to promote healing between people or a fulfillment of unmet obligations. They are the consequence of transgressing cultural and family taboos and the resultant dread of punishment and censure that follow.

Existential guilt relates to the sense and quest for justice that all of us have in some way, a sense that is often denied or minimized. Only the person who has never suffered because of feeling unfairly treated or who has never rebelled against injustice can deny that justice is a fundamental issue in human relationships. Although the world is far from being fair and people often expect fairness when it is impossible, most of us are touched deeply by the issue of justice. Family members keep an implicit accounting of justice, of obligations met or failed, of responsibilities fulfilled or neglected, of how much has been given and how much received from one's family. A quest for achieving justice, for striking a balance of fairness between oneself and one's relationships, underlies much of our motivation. In the lives of children perhaps nothing is so sharply honed as a sense of justice.

Because it confronts parents and children with their reciprocal obligations and responsibilities, existential guilt is important and constructive. It is also an unavoidable issue, although it may be rarely if ever discussed openly. Our society does too little to call parents to the accountability they incur when they give life to their offspring and too little to remind children that they owe something to their parents in return.

On the other hand, neurotic guilt feelings militate against personal growth and individual accountability. They can bind together a destructive marriage, block a child from being emotionally independent from his or her family, or handicap a separated parent from establishing a new and satisfying life-style.

Neurotic guilt feelings in a child can arise as a reaction to divorce and as a function of disturbed family relatedness. Parents cultivate guilt feelings in their children when they blame them for the separation. As an excuse for their own marital failure or personal mistakes, parents may imply to the child that he or she was never wanted or was the financial or emotional burden that destroyed the marriage.

Caught in the throes of a loyalty conflict where he or she is forced to take sides, a child feels guilty toward the rejected parent. That child is deprived of the opportunity to maintain loyalty ties to both parents. The child can also feel neurotically guilty toward the custodial parent if he or she has a better time with the noncustodial parent during visitation, times that are often dedicated to the pursuit of fun. The child finds false security in denying parental fallibility and blaming himself or herself for the family conflict. As I said before, anger and resentment are common reactions to divorce and custody conflicts. These feelings can provoke guilt feelings in a child, particularly in families where these feelings are suppressed and interdicted.

Parents incur existential guilt when they injure their children through their chronic battles over custody, their preoccupation with revenge toward the former spouse, their neglect of their children's needs, or their consideration of the children as burdens to be endured or restrictions to be resented. Children incur existential guilt when they refuse to show their parents some fair consideration — expressed by helpful, positive actions — for what they have been given.

Reconciliation Preoccupations

Not all children want their parents to stay together. The level of family strife can be so high that separation comes as a relief. The departure of a cruel, abusive, or rejecting parent can be welcomed. Probably a majority of children, however, hope that their parents stay together. Even though life at home can be distressing, it is familiar and therefore preferable to the new life, which is unknown. Most children yearn for a stable home life in which their needs will be met, their lives secure, and their competencies nurtured.

Preoccupation with reconciliation is not just part of a child's psychological makeup; parents often actively contribute to these thoughts. A divorce does not necessarily mean that parents have dissolved their emotional ties. A malevolent emotional relationship between divorced parents, one characterized by chronic hostility, contributes to reconciliation fantasies in children. Paradoxically, fighting connotes caring, or at least interest. Children sense that their parents who fight with each other are still emotionally involved. Otherwise, apathy would prevail.

Out of mutual dependency, other parents fail to emotionally separate. A benevolent relationship between parents, one in which they meet occasionally, possibly have sex together, perhaps talk about getting back together but are never able to do so, fans a child's preoccupation with reconciliation. Or one parent, hoping for a reconciliation, uses custody or visitation as a pretext for keeping the uninterested spouse involved or for trying to draw that person back into the marriage. Acting through the child, the parent who wants a reconciliation tries to reinvolve the estranged mate.

Reactions Depending on a Child's Age

This section is mostly a summary of research findings. For more detailed information the reader is referred to the following articles: Wallerstein and Kelly (1974a, 1974b, 1976a, 1976b); Kelly and Wallerstein (1977)*; Rohrlich et al. (1977); Henning and Oldham (1977). The categories refer to developmental stages rather than to precise, chronological ages.

Infants (up to Two Years)

Theoretical indications, not research findings, suggest that the danger for infants in divorce is the disruption in the stability and security of the infant's world because of the problems of the primary caretaker. Overwhelmed or depressed, the

---

*Some of their research is now contained in a book: Wallerstein, Judith S. and Kelly, Joan Berlin, *Surviving the Breakup — How Children and Parents Cope with Divorce* (New York: Basic Books, 1980).

custodial parent can lack sufficient resources to care for the infant properly. This can result in disorders of sleeping, eating, and eliminating, as well as causing irritability and resistance to comfort.

As the custodial parent returns to the job market to begin working or to work longer hours, as leisure time is filled with attempts to rebuild a social life now that the parent is single, less time and energy is available for raising children. Children begin their struggle for autonomy between one and two years of age. At this age children are frequently provocative. Already overwhelmed, parents can react negatively to their children's behavior by becoming permissive, negligent, demanding, or restrictive. What is actually needed are firm but reassuring outer controls to help the child master his or her inner drives.

Preschoolers (Three to Five Years)

From the end of infancy until about age five or six, children have an incomplete and confused understanding of what has caused such a radical upheaval in their lives and family routines. On account of cognitive limitations, in which they view the world egocentrically, children believe that events refer to them, that happenings are caused by them. Consequently they tend to feel responsible and guilty for a divorce; something or other has happened and they caused it. In some ways they are aware of a loss but lack sufficient capacity to cope with it and make sense out of it. Their symptoms include regression (enuresis, elimination and sleeping problems), aggressive behavior, irritability, tantrums, depression, loss of self-esteem, sadness, impaired self-image, and fears of abandonment (that they will lose their rooms, toys, furniture, parents, and security). Preschoolers require continual reassurance to counteract fears of being abandoned. They need to know that the custodial parent at least will take care of them in the future, that he or she will return from work or a date, that the parent's new spouse or lover will not usurp the place of the child's absent parent.

Early Latency (Seven to Eight Years)

With this stage comes entry into school and more peer-related activities. Children begin to move out of the boundaries of their homes and into the surrounding social world. Peer group norms take on greater importance. Children of divorce feel vulnerable to unfavorable comparisions with those of their peers who still have both parents at home.

Although it is true at any age, a child in early latency especially needs to be free of preoccupation with family and parental conflict so that an investment of self in school and peer activity can take place. A child's emerging autonomy, moreover, needs time to develop, whereas intense involvement in parental conflicts interferes with this. Early latency children feel literally split in two if they are required to take sides between their parents (loyalty conflicts). They are subject to intense fears about the future and about the instability of their home life. Feeling a sense of loss, they become sad and express their anxieties through possessiveness and preoccupation with fantasies of reconciliation.

An early latency child can try to cope with insecurity and felt deprivation by demanding new clothes and new toys. Through magical thinking, such a child can distort the image of his or her absent parent. The parent reinforces this by coming to visit bearing gifts and surprises and being with the child only for brief periods of play and recreation. An early latency child might be propagandized by a custodial parent who disparages the absent parent. In either case the child lacks sufficient intellectual and emotional sophistication to arrive at an independent, objective judgment of either parent.

Late Latency (Nine to Ten Years)

Intense anger directed at one or both parents, disciplinary problems, shame, and loneliness characterize late latency children's reaction to divorce. Unlike younger children, these children actively struggle to cope with the turbulence of divorce and their intense and conflicted feelings about it. Mechanisms of defense are likely to be denial, bravado, and avoidance activity. The intense anger they feel is exhibited in temper tantrums, excessive demands, and dictatorial attitudes. In addition to anger, loneliness, shame, and fear, other reactions are common, including somatic symptoms and poor school performance.

Adolescence

To adolescents, divorce can be excruciating, arousing anger at parents, sadness, a sense of betrayal, shame, embarrassment, and anxiety about their own futures in being adequate marital and sexual partners. Adolescence should be the dawning of emotional independence from parents. Autonomy, however, does not come smoothly nor all at once; it takes place in fits and starts, with hesitant steps, with conflicting attitudes and feelings, and inconsistent behavior. Unlike preschoolers, adolescents do not usually feel personally responsible for divorce. Nevertheless, their developing independence can be derailed by involvement in parental conflict. Adolescents can be parentified with family burdens. Divorce can accelerate their movement toward adulthood, often prematurely. In other cases, an adolescent forms an alliance with one parent against the other.

To cope with divorce, adolescents turn to distancing behavior, such as increased social activity, or withdrawal, or staying away from home a lot. With highly vulnerable adolescents, divorce provokes more serious symptoms: sexual acting out, drug abuse, drinking, regression. Adolescents do best if from the start they establish emotional distance from parental conflict with parental approval to do this. Sometime after a divorce, many adolescents gain empathy for their parents' struggles. With greater cognitive, emotional, and social competence, adolescents can arrive at independent appraisals of their parents, seeing them as individuals, not just as a unit. Adolescents are also able to meet their needs in alternative ways, so they are not as dependent on what their parents do, as are younger children.

SUMMARY

Confronted with a separation, divorce, and intense custody conflict, children have different reactions depending upon their ages and developmental stages, individual personalities, and family relationships. Temporary reactions — which include anger, depression, somatic symptoms, acting out, regression, excessive demands for attention, anxiety, and guilt — are common and should be transitory unless the pattern of family interactions undermines a child's loyalties and developmental strivings, or unless a child was highly vulnerable in the first place. Then these otherwise transitory reactions become persistent conflicts. The first year or so after a separation seems to be particularly stressful for a family.

The degree of symptomatic behavior for a child is a function of a child's prior development and adjustment, the parent-child relationship of both parents before and after a divorce, and the parent-parent relationship and whether or not a child is inappropriately involved in that interaction.

Divorce makes all children emotionally vulnerable and at high risk. Bitter, fiercely contested custody suits raise the potential for psychological damage. Children's different reactions to a divorce have to do with their developmental stage. Theoretically, infants tend to react with sleeping, eating, or elimination problems if the security of their world is disrupted due to the adjustment problems of their primary caretakers. Research findings give us information about older children. Feeling personally at fault for divorce, preschoolers can feel guilty but be at a loss to cope with the upheaval in their lives. Early latency children experience fears about their futures and the stability of their home life. In late latency, anger, shame, and loneliness dominate, but these children actively try to cope with their intense and conflicted feelings. Although they do not usually feel responsible for a divorce, adolescents find divorce to be extremely painful. They react with anger, sadness, shame, and a feeling of betrayal. Those adolescents who are able to establish emotional distance from their parents' conflicts — and whose parents allow them to do this — adjust the best.

Children at any developmental stage are subject to loyalty conflicts which in my opinion are the greatest dangers they confront.

FOUR

Children's Needs

WHAT ARE THE NEEDS OF children as their families go through a separation and a custody and visitation determination?

PSYCHOLOGICAL NEEDS: LOVE, STIMULATION, FEELING IMPORTANT

Every child needs a secure, stable relationship with an affectionate and stimulating adult (Goldstein et al., 1973). From such a relationship comes trust, the cornerstone of all future development and relationships. Erikson (1963, 1968) wrote that trust exists when a child comes to rely on the sameness and continuity of a caretaker. Trust, which engenders faith and hope, is also a trust in oneself, in the capacity of the self to cope with instinctual urges, including sexual and aggressive impulses. Erikson considers trust a virtue in the sense that it is an inherent human strength and an active quality that gives a child vitality and hope. For a child and for an adult trust is present when the inside and outside are experienced as good and as reliable.

Sullivan (1940, 1953) helped us understand children's physical and emotional requirements. He wrote that children's most basic needs are the pursuit of satisfaction and the maintenance of security. Satisfaction refers to the fulfilling of biological and physical needs necessary for maintaining life.

Children need to have their bodies tended to, nourished, and protected. The maintenance of security means freedom from excessive interpersonal anxiety, so that a child's self-esteem and self-image can be built and preserved.

Emotionally, children need to have people to love and to be loved by. They need safe targets for their infantile urges of aggression, people with whom they can be angry without destroying the relationship. They also need to be helped to direct their primitive drives (including sex and aggression) into socially acceptable outlets, expressions that allow for the uniqueness and creativity of their own personalities. Children rely on adults, usually their parents, for models for identification, for acquiring patterns for behavior, for learning how to become men and women, how to love and how to get angry, how to assert their rights without disregarding those of others, how to choose a career and make commitments, how to pursue the truth and live by it once it is known. Children look to their parents for well-defined limits and values, a context in which they can test out behaviors and know for certain what is expected of them.

Cognitive stimulation is also needed. Children require help in understanding their world and organizing their perceptions. A stimulating relationship with an adult alerts them to the happenings in their environment. Cognitive development is essential because it underlies the growth of the capacity to make moral judgments. Not only do children learn values from their parents; they also acquire the ability to come to decisions about the worth of their actions. Piaget (1965) and later Kohlberg (1963, 1968) studied moral judgment in detail.

A child starts out a strict moralist, believing that duty is unchanging and unswerving. To do good is to rigidly obey, and the morality of obedience is strict and blind. Although sacred and unchangeable, parental rules seem external to the child, and do not transform conduct. The child respects rules as unalterable but practices them as arbitrary. Justice, so important and so keenly felt, is at first the exact letter of the law, not its spirit or intention.

Children between the ages of eight and ten years continue to develop cognitively and socially and experience a shift in their thinking and moral judgments. They begin to understand situations from various points of view. Rules become changeable and can be followed with understanding and not just with mindless adherence. Based on equity and reciprocity, justice and fairness begin to hold sway over thoughtless obedience.

Children and adults are not the same cognitively and emotionally. Unlike adults who are able to delay gratification, children have more urgent instinctual and emotional needs that press for fulfillment. Lengthy separations from caretakers become disruptive and extremely taxing. The capacity to plan for the future and to delay action in the present is not yet developed in young children. Piaget (1965) noted that not until about thirteen or fourteen years do children acquire the ability for the type of thinking that he calls "formal operations": for anticipating the consequences of decisions, and for raising hypotheses about the world around them, and for finding ways to verify or disregard these hunches.

Adults differ from children in that they can find substitute gratification when their needs are not met by one situation or by one person. Adults can learn to use creative solutions to problems, instead of repeating old unsuccessful ones. Admittedly, we all repeat many of our mistakes, but at least the capacity is there to learn from experience and to overcome apparent limitations.

More than children, adults are able to prioritize values and choose from among various options to fulfill their needs. For instance, humans have crucial biological needs, including food, shelter, sex, and nurturance. Sometimes, however, adults postpone the fulfillment of these needs to attend to certain responsibilities (being a parent, for one) and to pursue other interests (such as art and literature, science and philosophy, social welfare and politics). Bound more to short-term pleasures and immediate goals, children tend to seek out self-centered gratification.

Cognitively and emotionally, children are more egocentric than adults. In a sense, before the age of seven or eight, a child lives in a world of his or her own, shut up within the confines of a limited point of view. It is a world bounded by cognitive limitations on one side, devoid of the capacity to recognize long-term consequences and cause-effect relationships, and circumscribed on the other side by a narrow social world, the inability to see life from someone else's perspective, and by urgent instinctual needs that bring on severe anxiety when frustrated. Children believe that events refer solely to them, that things occur only for their benefit or detriment. Separation can be seen as a personal rejection, and the death of a parent as abandonment. Young children assume that others view the world as they do.

Adults reason differently. They understand events as being determined by a complex interaction of circumstances. Although some refuse to acknowledge this, parents can know, for example, that a divorce is partially determined by each spouse and not their children's fault.

Adults can recognize, and to some extent tolerate, ambivalent feelings and conflicting motivation in themselves and others. Adults are able to anticipate the consequences of a decision. They can envision the future and recall the past and use that information in the present.

Adults learn to appreciate the intentions behind actions, whereas until about eight to ten years of age, children judge behavior strictly on the basis of consequences. Piaget (1965) explained that young children judge an accidental dropping of a tray of cups as worse than the deliberate breaking of one cup, because the physical consequences in the former are more serious than in the latter. Motivation or intention holds little relevance for them.

Children are governed more by their irrational wishes, impulses, and fantasies and less by rational thinking. Even in adulthood, this issue may never be resolved. Bowen (1978) has made the "differentiation of self" one of the fundamental tenets in his theory of family functioning and therapy. He has distinguished the relatively well differentiated person from the poorly differentiated one. In the former, thinking processes are clearly distinguished from feeling states. The well-differentiated person makes decisions on the basis of well-thought-out conclusions and important life principles. In the latter, feelings dominate one's life. Because decisions are based on what feels good, the individual has trouble differentiating opinions from emotional reactions and facts and evidence from feelings. Under stress, poorly differentiated people set reason aside and try to solve problems with emotional responses.

Since children lack a realistic perspective in which to understand their problems, they react to threats to their security with fantastic anxiety, distortion, the displacement of feelings onto inappropriate objects, and reversals, meaning that instead of acknowledging fear they pretend to be brave. None of these reactions aids in coping. When we understand this, it is easy to appreciate some of the reactions of children mentioned in chapter 3.

The significance of being wanted and important to at least one person, and of being intimately related to a family in which commitment and devotion are prized, has been emphasized by many, including Helm Stierlin (1976), a psychoanalytic family therapist. For a person to be important to himself or herself it is first necessary to be found important to someone else. The capacity to be important to yourself, to own up to your inner life, which ultimately depends on being "owned" or valued by others, encompasses several dimensions. It includes the capacity for self-object differentiation, in which one's own personal feelings, opinions, and thoughts are distinguished from those of others, and in which personal responsibilities are differentiated from those of other people. It includes gaining a sense of being at home in one's own body and of having trust in oneself. It means learning to recognize and tolerate ambivalent feelings within oneself. Implied in it is the willingness to own up to the truth of one's experience and inner life, especially the sinister aspects of one's personality — greed, revenge, hatred, and avarice, to name a few.

A child does not begin life with these capacities. And unless a child is important to someone and highly valued, the development of these features will be in jeopardy. Stierlin speaks of "wayward youth" (1976, p. 287), those who have been cut loose too early from the family. These are the youth that have not so much been abused as neglected, abandoned, and never bound to a caring family. Never being given a task or direction in life, a constructive mission to fulfill, these youth have literally been "turned away," put out of the family before they had the maturity to live independently. They lack a commitment to society, since no caretakers made commitments to them. Not bound to principles, laws, or commitments, they follow their own caprices. Only a child who has been bound in a constructive way and held accountable, who is important to at least one adult, can in turn value others and engage in mature, reciprocal interpersonal relationships.

THE NEED TO BE TREATED FAIRLY

Beside emotional and cognitive needs, there are also needs pertaining to the ethical dimension of relationships. This means a child needs to be treated fairly and to be taught to treat others fairly (Boszormenyi-Nagy and Spark, 1973).

There are many ways for children to be unfairly treated. A child should not be overindulged, so that the immediate gratification of needs becomes a single-minded concern throughout life. A child also needs to learn reciprocity and fairness in relationships, to be given enough freedom to pursue personal goals but also to be held accountable to consider the rights and feelings of others in return.

Parents are accountable to raise their children to maturity, but they should expect some fair, age-appropriate consideration in return. Overgiving, in the sense of never allowing a child to give back for what he or she has received, and overcaring, in the sense of doing for a child what the child can and should do for himself or herself, are far from the ideal of good parenting. Rather they hide a parent's true dependency on a child.

Perhaps parentification, mentioned in chapter 1, is the most common form of unfair treatment of children. A parentified child is made unfairly accountable for someone else, either a parent or another child. Parentification takes place when a parent continually relies on and acts toward a child as if that child was actually a parent.

Children can be parentified in terms of dependency; then they are emotionally needed by their parents, who rely on them for the bulk of their emotional support. It should be reiterated that any parent should derive satisfaction from a child, but parentification is an excessive dependency that exhausts a child's coping capacities and interferes with development. Incest parentifies a child sexually. A child can also be the target of parental rage and violence, leading to parentification in an aggressive way; usually the parent is discharging pent-up anger that originated in his or her relationship with one or both parents, but because of loyalty or a lack of opportunity, those feelings cannot be expressed directly. In therapy, such an individual would benefit from learning the difficulties his or her parent may have had that led to the neglect or abuse. Then a lessening of anger is possible. And a child can be functionally parentified when he or she is given excessive and inappropriate responsibilities at home without parental supervision.

All forms of parentification exploit children because they

hinder a child's cognitive, social, and emotional development. Since they inappropriately involve a child in his or her
parent's life, they ask the child to give more to the parent than
the parent gives to the child.

Scapegoated children are victims of family exploitation,
although many children willingly accept this designation.
These children are blamed for the breakup of the marriage,
thus hiding the parents' own contributions and failings. Children are sometimes rejected or neglected because their parents feel they are too burdensome, too expensive, or too restrictive. This is another variation of exploitation.

In bitter, competitive custody suits children are commonly
used for their parents' own personal ends. They can be used as
pawns in a battle of revenge between spouses. Custody may
be sought not so that a child's needs are assured, but as a sign
of power for the "winning" parent, as the spoils of victory, or
as a measure of self-worth, self-esteem, or self-vindication.
Children are exploited when they are used as message carriers
or go-betweens in their parents' struggles. These and other
forms of exploitation will be explored more fully in the next
chapter.

A child is treated fairly only if he or she is loved for himself
or herself, not on account of accomplishment, looks, or
earned merit, that is, what a child can do for a parent. Finally
children are treated fairly when they are taught to treat their
siblings fairly, too.

CONSTRUCTIVE LOYALTIES

The viability of a child's relationship with his or her family requires the fulfillment of another urgent although invisible need: the preservation of constructive loyalty ties
(Boszormenyi-Nagy and Spark, 1973). Constructive loyalty
means that a child is able to love both parents simultaneously
and is expected to become a mature, responsible individual.
Young children have severe problems loving more than one

significant adult unless that adult feels positively toward the other adult (Goldstein et al., 1973). It is perplexing and extremely difficult for a young child to simultaneously love two parents who are battling and vilifying each other in a divorce or custody suit. Older children and adolescents gain the capacity to esteem both parents despite marital strife, but this situation also invites serious loyalty problems.

Caught in the vise of divided or split loyalties, where loyalty to one parent equals disloyalty to the other, a child feels conflicted and his or her loyalties sabotaged. In such a situation a child can bounce back and forth between parents, living with one until guilt feelings in reference to the other become too intense. Or a child may enter into a coalition with one parent against the other and always have a distorted view of both parents and of the nature of the marital problems and the causes of divorce.

There is a worse form of loyalty problem for a child, one that may harm him or her for life. I am referring to what Boszormenyi-Nagy and Spark term negative loyalty, when the personal failure of a child in some way helps a parent or family. Only by failing is a child able to show loyalty to the family. An example is a parent who needs to have a child remain emotionally a child for life or for an extended period of time in order to always have someone to take care of. Certain psychotic or schizophrenic youths are extreme examples of this. A child who stays home from school to care for an alcoholic parent or one who gets into trouble as a way of distracting a depressed parent away from the parent's personal problems are further instances.

If growing up emotionally means disloyalty and forebodes a painful separation for the parent, a child may be encouraged to remain forever dependent, immature, and incompetent. Thus, a child's failure to leave home emotionally (not necessarily physically) may be the only available expression for his or her loyalty to the family and parent. A child stays loyal, but at his or her own personal expense, that is, negatively.

The above needs — to have a constructive way to be loyal to the family, to be treated fairly, to be loved and wanted, to be stimulated and found important — are extensive. Few if any families meet all of them. It is more a question of relative balance on the side of meeting needs rather than frustrating them.

Many factors impinge on whether or not parents can meet their children's needs. Under the strain of a divorce and in the throes of a custody or visitation contest, the ability to parent effectively is reduced or at least put to a severe test.

First of all, there are reality stresses for parents. Divorce means financial hardship; both parents may have to work, if they didn't already, or work full-time instead of part-time. Cultural attitudes sometimes disparage single-parent families, so that divorced or separated parents feel isolated and alone. Extended families can withdraw support from parents during these difficult times.

A second crucial determination of parents' ability to meet their children's needs is the current status of the marital relationship. Because divorce does not guarantee an end to an emotional relationship, parents with unresolved emotional attachments to each other, whether based on animosity, ambivalent feelings, or dependency, may be too involved in these issues to adequately respond to their children.

A third factor refers to the parents having been adequately parented in their own families of origin. Adults whose psychological, cognitive, and relationship needs were neglected in childhood frequently feel emotionally bankrupt and therefore unable to meet their children's needs. The stress of a divorce and custody contest further depletes them.

Individual factors in a child can militate against the fulfillment of basic needs. Children with developmental lags, neurotic problems, or emotional symptoms are difficult enough
to handle. As noted in chapter 3, a divorce or custody battle
tends to trigger problematical reactions — including denial,
anger, somatic symptoms, anxiety, behavioral disorders,
sleeping or eating problems, compulsions and phobias, depression, grief, regression, greater dependency, and increased
demands. These reactions often push a parent away, and the
parent's withdrawal heightens the child's reactions, thus com-
pleting a vicious circle.

The availability of support systems, a fifth variable, is important for parents. Supportive friends and relatives are salutary during divorce. Sometimes the help of agencies, such as
day-care centers, community mental health clinics, or formal
support groups for parents, are invaluable. Without them
parents feel more alone and will probably be even less emotionally prepared to meet their children's needs.

Adversary legal proceedings bring about greater strife and
conflict and decrease the chances of parents working out constructive solutions to the custody or visitation issues. Whereas
my approach is to attempt to unite the couple as parents (not
as spouses) in order to work out suitable custody and visitation
arrangements, the legal process frequently pits one parent
against the other and thereby undermines any chance at a
compromise.

A seventh factor is the involvement of the extended families. Sometimes grandparents, siblings, and other family
members become just as embroiled in the divorce and custody
problems as the divorcing couple. Their involvement can discourage parents from resolving their differences, which
should be done at least for the sake of the children. Since
loyalty to the family of origin can preclude appropriate loyalty to the nuclear family, cooperation with a former spouse
under these circumstances becomes very difficult. I have seen

a grandparent just as angry at the other spouse as is his or her own child. Finally, throughout the entire family, the greater the emotional reactiveness that displaces clearheaded thinking, the less likely a constructive, viable, and fair resolution will be reached.

SUMMARY

Divorce and custody contests make the needs of children more urgent and more difficult to satisfy. They are more urgent because the tremendous upheaval associated with the breakup of the family jeopardizes children emotionally. They are more difficult to satisfy since embittered custody contests mean embittered family relationships which exploit children. It is difficult for parents to be loving when they are struggling to adjust to a separation or when they are still embroiled with a former spouse. And when custody becomes the parents' way of revenging each other or fulfilling personal needs, children are seriously neglected and exploited. The absence of support systems, adversary legal proceedings, and anger in the parents' extended families exacerbate the problem.

What are these needs? Only when children are loved and wanted will they develop trust in the world and confidence in themselves. Meeting their needs for physical safety and emotional security encourages self-esteem. Children need guidance in order to become masters of themselves and cognitive stimulation so that they can develop a capacity for moral judgment and grow out of their natural cognitive and emotional self-centeredness. By being important to another person, they are helped to accept themselves as a mixture of positive and negative traits and to value others as well as themselves.

Since custody contests push children aside, fairness in parent-child relationships becomes a paramount issue during these times. Children need sufficient love in order to mature, but they should also be expected to treat their parents and siblings fairly in return. Parents ought to regard children as children, not as small adults, surrogate parents or partners, scapegoats, or burdens; as important individuals deserving respect, not for what advantages they can provide their parents through custody.

Finally, children need to be protected from becoming pawns in their parents marital battles, so that constructive loyalties to both parents are preserved. And children should have positive ways of expressing loyalty, not ways that interfere with their emotional growth.

FIVE

Contested Custody Cases

IN ATTEMPTING TO UNDERSTAND WHAT happens to children involved in a divorce and custody or visitation controversy, my premise is that a child is an individual, but an individual who belongs to a family; a child is not understood unless his or her family is understood as well. And a family is a system that has its own history. Over generations a family develops rules for its members regarding their interaction with each other and with the outside world. These rules help to define what is acceptable or unacceptable, what is true or false about themselves and the world, what is fair and unfair in the family, what loyalty to the family demands and what loyalty prohibits.

Every child is at high risk during a divorce and especially during a custody or visitation disagreement, but no child is necessarily damaged. What constitutes a child's vulnerability is an urgent issue for therapists, parents, judges, attorneys, educators, and for society itself.

To understand a child's vulnerability, it is not enough to appreciate the child as a specific individual, with one or more reactions or symptoms. Nor is it enough to understand that children at different ages tend to have characteristic reactions. It is also inadequate simply to identify the needs of any child as his or her parents divorce: for each child is sustained

71

by a secure relationship with a loving adult; each child must have stimulation and a sense of being wanted and valued; each child should be treated fairly and not exploited, and have loyalty ties to both parents protected.

To understand what happens to children during custody conflicts requires insight into the particular family relationship system in which a child lives and through which those needs are met or neglected, a system characterized by constructive or exploitative relationships. Essential, too, is a cognizance of the specific role or position a child plays in the parental interaction and the motivations parents have for seeking custody.

This chapter explores the various roles a child can assume in his or her parents' relationship as they battle for custody. In order to set the context of the discussion, we will look at some of the historical and psychological forces that are shaping and are shaped by the family today. This discussion is by no means exhaustive, but merely an introduction to a complex topic.

THE FAMILY TODAY

To say that history has become unstuck and that times are changing is commonplace. What is happening to the family in the United States in the midst of this provides a background and prelude to an understanding of what happens to children and their parents during custody conflicts.

As stated in the first chapter, not only are divorces increasing, but as a result, there is also a rise in single-parent families. An increasing number of children live at least part of their lives with only one parent. Whatever the reasons for this, several factors should be noted. I am not suggesting that there is a direct, causal relationship between these factors and divorce and custody problems, but only that they are influencial and are some of the relevant issues that need to be taken up.

Rapid social change, including increased mobility, frequent changes of employment, rapid transit, global communication, and the realization that the world is deeply interdependent regarding energy and food bring with them a narrowing of our world on the one hand, but there is also a sense of isolation of the nuclear family today on the other hand. Often removed from an extended family — adults separated from their parents and siblings, children from their grandparents, aunts, and uncles — extended family ties are threadbare for many people. As a result, more is expected from the nuclear family, and a greater strain is placed on all family members. Any adult with children who is cut off from his or her nuclear family feels this acutely when there are no grandparents or siblings to help with child-rearing and baby-sitting. A divorce augments this problem, because then the absence of a stable, supportive social network strikes even harder. After a divorce not even one's spouse is emotionally available, and sometimes he or she is not physically present to the children either.

The rising divorce rate testifies to the upheaval and changes in marriages today. The hopes and dreams of courtship frequently become the despair and disillusionment of later married life. In the "me" generation, and in an age of the isolated nuclear family, more is expected from married life. Disappointment is more often and more intense.

Unrealistic expectations about marriage also take their toll. In one sense, each of us at some time has searched for the all-loving, all-giving parent who will accept us despite our limitations and without reservations. Courtship and the early phase of marriage rekindle this hope, but no spouse can live up to these yearnings; certainly no one can make up for what a person missed while growing up.

It is a repeated experience in marital therapy that people sometimes seek out a spouse who is just like one or both parents. Disappointment is inevitable, since no one can replace a parent and no one is an exact replica of a previous significant other. Psychotherapy also instructs us that men and women often select a mate who has one or more negative traits that belonged to a parent, a trait that they already disliked or hated. Perhaps the person is still trying to change the parent in the person of the spouse. Perhaps that person seeks out the familiar even though it is painful.

Bowen (1978) helped alert clinicians to the idea that some people marry seeking the ideal close relationship with a spouse. In such cases, each person expects excessive, unlimited devotion from the other, investing more energy in the relationship — seeking approval and avoiding rejection — than in any goal-directed behavior. Each spouse believes that the other, not the self, is responsible for personal happiness. These marriages are subject to great turmoil and distress, passing through cycles of closeness and distance, relative calm and angry disillusionment.

Nor should utopian notions about marriage be overlooked as we reflect on the turbulence in marriages today. For some couples, any conflict means a loss of love; outside interests equal rejection; togetherness demands never being separate; differences connote excessive emotional distance. These ideas interfere with a healthy balance in a relationship between enough togetherness to achieve intimacy but sufficient separateness to accomplish self-reliance.

An acceptance of different life-styles influences today's family. Being single is a choice rather than a case of being left out. As being a single parent, whether through divorce or adoption, gains acceptance, it brings with it serious responsibilities. Cohabitation is gaining in popularity, but such relationships are more easily dissolvable, at least legally; they lack the same institutional constraints and supports that marriages have. Children from these unions or from previous marriages can grow up with a series of parents and caretakers, the impact of which is not yet understood.

The women's rights movement is helping to alter the interaction between men and women. Many women demand equal opportunity in the work force and freedom of choice for personal fulfillment paralleling that allowed to men. Both of these are based on emotional and financial independence. Women in greater numbers are asking for freedom of options regarding personal roles: to stay home in the traditional role of homemaker or take up a professional career. Women are also enunciating their freedom of choice regarding child-rearing and motherhood.

Finally, attitudes toward child-rearing are changing. Joint custody has arrived as an idea (Roman and Haddad, 1978), although the advisability and practicality of it needs greater study, and the use of it in judicial decisions is not prevalent so far. More men seek custody today and although many may not seek or gain custody, more men recognize their importance and competence in raising children.

CUSTODY/VISITATION BATTLES

Custody and visitation conflicts take place when parents consciously or unconsciously put their needs ahead of their children's, or when one or both parents are unable to separate from each other emotionally and so use custody or visitation to achieve some advantage or some personal objective in the marital relationship. In such contests children fall victim to a variety of roles.

The Child as Parent

Children usually cooperate in being parentified. On one level, a parentified child is angry and possibly depressed. A child may try to reject this designation, but loyalty to the family is strong, and a sense of being needed by the family gratifies the child, who, on another level, accepts and encourages the parentification.

Parentified means taking on parental responsibilities or duties to the detriment of a child's personal growth. The child becomes like a parent in the family. Parentified children are given the message that their parents depend on them as if they, not the parents, were the adults or decision makers. Some parents seek out custody so that their children will be obliged and available to take care of them now and in old age.

An example from a family I counseled illustrates parentification. A sixteen-year-old was charged with taking care of his three younger brothers, since his mother was too anxious and upset to parent effectively. A marital separation had occurred three years before, but the parents still fought regularly, especially about the "welfare" of the children. This adolescent would try to break up his parents' fights and calm them down. All the children lived with their mother. The parentified sixteen-year-old gave his mother personal and financial advice. In the custody evaluation the mother remarked that she would not marry again (once the divorce was final) until she first talked it over with this youth, her oldest son, and essentially got his approval. The sessions almost immediately deteriorated into an exchange of insults between the parents. In one session the parentified adolescent quickly interrupted his parents and told me that he was getting sick over the fighting and that the evaluation should be terminated immediately. He had become the parent in the family, the person who consoles, calms, gives advice, and sets limits for his parents. An anxious youth, he was "mature" before his time. About his family he remarked to me: "I have most of the responsibility."

After three sessions with this family, the parents agreed to stop arguing in front of the children and stop asking the children, especially the sixteen-year-old, which parent was right. Six months later, however, the court sent the family to see me again: the parents had reneged on their agreement. First, I reinforced the original compromise. Then I told them that their fighting signified deep mutual affection — they would not fight if they did not care about each other, and they do not stop because it is the only way they know to demonstrate their concern — and, naturally, I would not expect them to stop something that was positive. They left the office perplexed but calm. Whether this intervention served to quiet their battles momentarily or had any lasting effects is unknown since I have not had any further contact with them. But incisive and paradoxical statements can sometimes promote rapid changes in families (Selvini Palazzoli, M.; Boscolo, L.; Cecchin, G.; and Prata, G., 1978).

The Child as Surrogate Partner

Loneliness can be intense after a divorce. In the absence of a mate, some parents turn to one of the children as confidant and comforter, someone to talk to in order to relieve the pain of being alone. In becoming a substitute companion or partner, the child in one sense is asked to replace the absent spouse. Of course, no child can really achieve this. Although a child can be of some comfort to a parent, it is primarily the parent's responsibility to comfort and nurture a child. Extreme cases of this are incest when a child is so much a partner as to assume a sexual relationship with his or her parent.

When a child is given the role of surrogate partner, a parent wants custody because the child is being used to meet the parent's needs for companionship, whereas custody ought to be sought primarily as a way of living up to the parental responsibilities of caretaking and giving affection.

The Child as Weapon

In all of us there is a sensitivity to being treated unjustly. The breakup of a marriage and the custody or visitation proceedings often lead to bitter battles. Feeling hurt, parents want to get back at each other; they seek custody to gain revenge. This type of revenge is particularly destructive because the way of getting back is through the children. One or both parents use the child as a weapon to hurt the other spouse. Custody is sought to deprive the other spouse, not to provide for the children.

A typical example from my clinical work involved a young husband and father in his late twenties, who tried to gain custody of his two children, and his wife, who opposed him. He and his wife had been separated for several months. The evaluation began bitterly: she accused him of neglecting the children, and he excoriated her for allegedly sabotaging visitation. Several sessions later, however, he withdrew his custody petition. He was able to verbalize that he had wanted custody to provoke his wife, because she had left him for another man. In so many words he said that he was angry at her and knew that a custody battle would be the most effective way to get to her. This man acknowledged to himself and admitted to me and his former wife that he was motivated mostly by revenge. Most people, similarly motivated, are not able or willing to do this. Many say that they are seeking custody only for their children's welfare, but they act in ways that violate their children's best interests.

Another example concerns a wife who refused to allow visitation. Her husband had left her while he was having an extramarital affair. When he attempted visitation, she protested that the children were sick or uninterested. She would reproach him for leaving the family and being unconcerned with the children (and her). In spite of severe marital conflict, this man attempted to be a responsible father to his children, but his wife's grievance against him for leaving hampered him. The marriage, it should be noted, had been seriously dysfunctional for some time; both spouses contributed to its demise, although the husband made the final break. Feeling hurt and abandoned, the wife tried to deny visitation as her way of getting even. I believe it was also an attempt to reinvolve her husband in the marital relationship. But it failed. Again, the marital problems and the wife's seeking revenge relegated the children's needs to second place. Difficult as it is for many couples to separate without serious grievances and feelings of injury, the danger to children is that a custody or visitation dispute will become the method parents use to redress their grievances and heal their injuries.

We should keep in mind that no one spouse is wholly at fault for the marital problems, and that both spouses usually collude to bring about a divorce or custody contest. Vicious cycles or feedback loops (Weakland, 1976, p. 123) commonly intensify the competition. The anger of one spouse stimulates the hostility or withdrawal of the other, which then only provokes a greater urge for revenge. During a divorce emotional intensity and reactiveness proliferate. Prolonged and concentrated anxiety brings out pathology in relationships. The clinician's task is to reduce the level of anxiety and then to refocus the family onto parent-child responsibilities instead of husband-wife animosities. Then the parents can learn to work together as parents, or at least not actively undermine each other.

The Child as Pawn

Who makes what decisions, or who has control, is a key issue in any marriage. A struggle for control that began in the marital interaction and that probably helped void the marital relationship can continue into the custody or visitation proceeding. Refusing to give in, neither side compromises. Chronic conflict and intense bickering characterize these relationships. Giving in means giving up and a loss of self. Couples who use their children as pawns in their relationship battles have been unable to disengage emotionally from each other. Neither parent is willing to give in for fear that the other parent will gain some personal advantage. Defeat the other is the battle cry.

Custody and visitation of children should not be a question of winning and losing between parents since all family members lose in acrimonious custody contests. The question should be changed from which parent will win to how can both parents be accountable to their children and provide them, as much as possible, with love and affection, structure and limits, stimulation and meaning, and trust and fairness, while teaching them about commitment and reciprocity in human relationships.

The Child as Bargaining Chip

Some spouses do not equally want an end to their marriage. One or both can be unable to let go. Sometimes the spouse still involved fights over custody as a way of trying to reinvolve the uninterested spouse. The involved spouse reasons that by provoking guilt or exploiting the uninterested spouse's concern for the children, the marital relationship can be revived.

My experience in these cases is that usually it is the noncustodial parent, estranged from the other parent and the family, who seeks reinvolvement with the family and who suddenly comes back into the picture and makes an unrealistic claim for custody or visitation. The claim is usually disingenuous. On the surface, for instance, the petitioning parent seeks to acquire custody or change the visitation arrangement (or begin visitation) but underneath lies a disguised attempt to have contact with his or her mate, with the usually farfetched hope of a reconciliation.

The custodial parent, or the parent who is uninterested in restoring the marital relationship, may want nothing to do with the petitioning parent. He or she might have started a new life. The independence that comes with this frightens the other parent, who fears that the final emotional break is coming. Threatened, the involved parent reacts by gratuitously seeking custody or changing visitation. It is a last chance to save the relationship, prompted by a need to control, or a fear of being alone and beginning a new life-style.

The Child as Trophy

The feeling of being a failure prompts some parents into trying to gain custody. Being the custodial parent becomes the benchmark of personal success and the foundation of self-esteem. Custody is not viewed as being in the best interests of the children or as the least detrimental alternative available, but as the fulfillment of a need for approval or self-aggrandizement. As best, the individual gains a false security.

In family systems terms, these parents and children are fused together (Bowen, 1978), and the family relationships enmeshed (Minuchin, 1974). Lacking sufficient self-other boundaries, goal directed behavior, and other sources of satisfaction, these parents devote excessive time, energy, and interest to their children. The child becomes the measure of a parent's inner worth; obtaining custody becomes the outward sign of that worth.

A clinical example will illustrate. A twenty-one-year-old father, separated from his nineteen-year-old wife, presented himself along with his wife for the court-ordered family evaluation because of the contested custody of their two-year-old son. He described himself as "an outcast," "depressed," "a born loser"; he felt that his son was "the only thing I have in life." In terms of his family of origin, he felt rejected by his parents and wanted custody so he could give to his son what he himself had missed, not realizing that this was an irresponsible way of trying to meet his son's needs. His own mother died when he was three and his father put him and his eight brothers and sisters into foster homes or institutions. As this young man phrased it, he was "put on the state." Feeling abandoned and angry, he grew up distant from people and distrustful, but unable to acknowledge his deep-seated dependency needs. As a way of meeting his own needs, he sought custody. In giving to his son he felt on some level that he was really giving to himself, to the child in him who still yearned for unconditional love and who was still very much a part of his life. He parentified his son by depending on the child emotionally for the major, if not only, source of satisfaction in his isolated life. As a father he derived the only meaning he had. Although he worked and lived with a woman, only his contact with his son gave him any satisfaction or purpose, he told me. Every week he looked forward to his visitation, and without it he felt lonely, depressed, and deprived.

This man's sense of justice had been severely injured. Over-giving and overreliance on his young son hid his own feelings of rejection, anger, worthlessness, and abandonment. He tried to give to his son as if he himself was the recipient of his devotion and ministrations. Weekend visits with his son were spent in buying sprees and games.

The evaluation and short-term counseling failed to help him reevaluate his position. His wife, who had adequately maintained custody since the separation and who was included in the evaluation, attempted to reassure him that he could count on regular visitation and free access to their son and that she would continue to care for the boy responsibly. Blinded by his own needs, the father was too deeply involved in obtaining custody to consider any alternative. The court awarded the custody to the mother and visitation to him.

The Child as Rescuer

In some cases one parent completely abandons the family after a separation. Although this may be provoked by both parents, the children are left completely without one parent. Financial problems and emotional distress confront the abandoned spouse, who has to carry on as a single parent without any help from the other spouse. Consciously or unconsciously, the individual comes to feel that there is no way to engage the non-custodial parent in supporting the family or in relating to the children since his or her efforts have failed so far.

One child in the family senses the parent's distress and out of loyalty to the family, along with his or her own anxiety about the absence of the other parent, begins to act out or develop symptoms. In chapter 3 I gave the the example of a child who threatened suicide, seeing it as the only way to reengage his father in the family. This child had sensed that his mother needed the father's financial support and emotional involvement with the children (she may also have been ambivalent about the marital separation) and tried to rescue her, himself, and his siblings by threats of suicide.

The Child as Anxiety-Reliever

It is easier to worry about one's child than it is to face the painful facts of one's own life. An anxious parent tries to find some explanation for the source of anxiety. Since divorce is stressful and often brings about symptoms in children, a child presents a ready target. A parent may seize upon these symptoms and identify them as the cause of all the family's problems and the parent's personal distress. Finding a reason for the anxiety helps to lessen it, and localizing it in the child temporarily relieves the parent from facing his or her inner turmoil.

Society can inadvertently reinforce this process, because worrying about a child can be seen as a way of showing concern for the child's needs. The parent, however, is not meeting the child's genuine needs: a child needs time to work through painful feelings at his or her own pace. Since the parent's underlying motive is not the child's welfare but relief from personal anxiety and distress, again, parental gain outweighs a child's needs.

The Child as Guilt-Reliever

Some parents feel guilty for the marital failure, the breakup of the family, and for leaving their children with only one custodial parent. Leaving the marriage for personal reasons, perhaps for a lover, intensifies these feelings. A custody or visitation suit then becomes a search for alleviating guilt feelings.

Failed responsibilities should be met. But neurotic guilt feelings do nothing to promote parental accountability. Nor can they cement a broken marriage. On the other hand, existential guilt, the guilt incurred for failure to meet one's genuine responsibilities, can be constructive if the parent recognizes it, not in agony and torture, but in calm reflection and perseverance. Once acknowledged, existential guilt should lead a parent to repair, if possible, whatever damage or harm has occurred on account of his or her actions or omissions.

Exploitation strikes a child whose custody is sought because of a parent's neurotic guilt feelings. The child will recognize in some way that he or she is important to the parent for the parent's sake, not for himself or herself. Not a genuine affirmation of the child's self-esteem and intrinsic worth, the child is used to attempt to resolve a parent's problems.

The Child as Go-Between or Spy

Going to court does not necessarily resolve a marital conflict, which is an emotional and relationship problem. Parents can divorce without ever separating emotionally. In these cases, each spouse's investment in the other remains high.

A child who belongs to such a family can be pressed into carrying messages back and forth between parents during visitation. Although the child is not told directly to do this, the child is stuck together enough with the family — and loyal enough — to comply with parental desires. One or both parents keep abreast of the other through messages and information transmitted by the child.

A child can also act as a spy for one parent, who pumps the child for information regarding his or her spouse. Still emotionally invested in the marital relationship, one parent seeks to find out the details of the other's life, especially regarding finances, living arrangements, and romantic episodes.

As a go-between or spy, a child is thrown into a profound loyalty conflict because a spy takes up one parent's side in a coalition against the other parent. Entrapped in the web of parental intrigue, a message carrier may be truly loyal to neither parent.

The custody or visitation question may never be settled. Denying or minimizing their deep interest in each other, these parents never confront one another with the issues or dialogue to resolve them. As long as a child acts as a mediator, message carrier, or spy, the parents are spared a confrontation with each other, and until the parents disengage emotionally or otherwise resolve their problems, the child is tied to this role.

The Child as Judge and Jury

Bowen (1978) divides people into blamers and self-blamers. Blamers excuse themselves and accuse others. Self-blamers take on all of the responsibility for a problem. The reality of human relationships, including marriage, is that usually both spouses jointly contribute to the viability or dissolution of a marriage; no single individual does it alone and no one is completely blameless or blameworthy.

Heightened by a battle over custody or visitation, a divorce or separation is replete with anxiety. Feeling the need to assign blame, some parents ask their children directly or indirectly to decide which parent is right or wrong. Children then become the judge and jury of marital fault.

In evaluation sessions parents turn to their children to verify the good they have done and the evil the other parents are guilty of. It is common for parents to look at their children in the midst of a hostile marital exchange and ask them to say which story is true, which parent is virtuous, which parent has been more loving, more responsible, more considerate. Sometimes this is done indirectly when a parent looks for an approving glance or affirming gesture.

But children are not the judges of their parents. In a sense, no one can judge who was right or wrong in a marriage, for a marital relationship is an emotional system in which circular causality and reciprocal functioning take place. Each person and each relationship contributes to the overall functioning of a system.

SUMMARY

Not every custody or visitation dispute is prompted by dysfunctional family relationships or unresolved marital problems. Not every parent who seeks custody does so in an attempt to meet personal needs at the expense of the children. Parents can contest custody because they believe, rightly or wrongly, that they are more suited for custody than their spouses. In fact, one parent may be unfit in the sense of being involved with the children only for personal gain, neglectful, irresponsible, or suffering from serious emotional or behavorial problems. One of the parents identifies the child's needs and tries to fulfill them.

On the other hand, both parents may be fit for custody or feel better suited. They do not necessarily have to believe that the other parent is incapable. In these cases, custody is more easily resolved, since gaining custody does not carry with it the emotional reasons that it does when parents fight for custody for their own sakes and not for the welfare of their children. When parents are relatively responsible instead of self-serving, they are quicker to grasp that their fighting harms their children.

In my experience, the most common case is where genuine parental concern is mixed with one or more self-serving motives. If the clinician and the family can capitalize on the strengths in the family, on parental accountability, and on whatever agreements parents can reach, these factors can outweigh the dysfunctional motives discussed in this chapter. A resolution is then possible.

The position that a child occupies in the family — as a parent, substitute partner, weapon, pawn, bargaining chip, trophy, rescuer, guilt- or anxiety-reliever, go-between or spy, judge and jury — is determined partially by the parents' marital relationship and their motives for seeking custody, whether they are to have someone to depend on, to relieve feelings of loneliness or anxiety, to seek revenge, to gain control over each other, to build up self-esteem, to reinvolve a disengaged spouse, to relieve guilt feelings, to give information to or find out information about a spouse, to vindicate the self and accuse the other, or to hold onto a shaky marital relationship. With loyalty to the family and out of self-preservation, a child accepts one or more of the above roles. By this the child gains recognition and attention, and most importantly, a sense of meaning in life and a feeling of being needed.

The willingness of a child to adopt one or more of these roles makes it possible for the parents to continue the type of interaction that places the child in that position. The family, then, is truly a system: the motives and interaction of the parents influence what roles their children will take on, and the acceptance of these roles by the children makes possible their parents' continuing sagas of conflict, struggle, and enmeshment.

Several motives — revenge, control, involving an estranged spouse, excusing the self and blaming the other, exchanging information or spying — involve the advantage a parent will supposedly gain in the relationship with his or her spouse and in the divorce. Other motives — having someone to depend on, relieving loneliness, guilt, or anxiety, and building up self-esteem — pertain more to a parent's personal life and inner feelings and less to the marital relationship, although the marital and family relationships are surely implicated.

SIX

Parents Adjust to Divorce

NOT ONLY ARE CHILDREN acutely vulnerable during a divorce and custody dispute, but parents also face great anxieties and profound life-style changes. What happens to parents going through a divorce and struggling over custody or visitation problems and how they can adjust are the topics of this chapter.

DIVORCE AS A TRANSITION

Throughout the course of its life a family faces many transitions or crises. Crisis in this context does not necessarily mean a catastrophe; it means a significant change or a turning point, one that requires a new direction, a shift in course, or an alteration of structure. Of the many crises a family experiences throughout its life span, many are inevitable and natural: the birth of a child, the marriage of a member, when a member leaves home to enter the adult world, or when a member is lost through death.

Transitions are initiated by different situations (Minuchin, 1974, pp.99–105). First, there are developmental changes in family members. A child moves into adolescence, increasing his or her interaction with peers and broadening his or her social radius outside the family. The adolescent's developing sexuality—a qualitatively different experience of the self—

and intensified emotionality present the adolescent and his or her family with new forces to cope with and new issues to work out. As the rules for conduct change, the responsibility of the adolescent toward the family shifts, eventually confronting the adolescent with rejecting, accepting, or modifying parental and adult values. In later adolescence identity issues come forward. Not only is the adolescent thinking about new issues — emotionality, sexuality, values, self-identity — the adolescent is also thinking differently. In early adolescence the capacity to envision the future and remember the past develops. The consequences of a decision can be understood and weighed. Hypotheses about the world can be made and verified or discarded. It is the stage of intellectual development that Piaget calls "formal operations."

As a result of these changes during adolescence, the relationships between parents and adolescents call for redefinition. As adolescents seek and find greater autonomy, parents should entrust them with more freedom, but without cutting them loose too soon or holding on too tightly.

Similarly, when a parent reaches middle age, a crisis often appears. At this time parents may rethink their marital and personal lives. Confronted with the coming threat of old age and on account of it depression, some parents try to hold onto their children to reduce this threat. Others, tired of the marital relationship and longing for a different life, react to their children as burdens or obstacles to freedom, pushing them prematurely into the adult world. As a result of the crisis or transition in the parents' lives, children become bound to or expelled from their parents' orbits (Stierlin, 1973). If a transition is successfully negotiated, however, the parent-child relationship will be redefined in a new and constructive way. For example, old age later prompts parents to turn to their adult children for greater support for themselves and the family. Without a complete reversal of roles, adult children learn to care for their aged parents.

The inclusion or loss of a family member is another crisis or transition point; a prime example of this is divorce. Although no transition is easy, divorce foments high levels of stress. Divorce requires a change in family structure and relationships. Remember the analogy of the home heating system and thermostat in chapter 1. Divorce throws the entire system off course. It is equivalent to losing the roof or breaking all the windows, or losing the house's entire insulating material. Imagine the heating adjustment necessitated by any of these disturbances.

Divorce and Life-Style Changes

Divorce can be a catastrophe or a challenge. For most people it is some of both. That divorce is anxiety-producing and unnerving is difficult to deny. Holmes and Rabe (cited in Fisher, 1976) list it as the second most traumatic event in a person's life. Only the death of a spouse surpasses it.

Any significant transition is stressful; change and conflict go hand in hand. Divorce comes with its own urgencies: grief or mourning of the former love relationship, disengagement and emotional separation, the building up and integration of a new life-style, making new friends, and setting new goals for life. Divorce is not an end to the family, but a severe change in its structure. For children, divorce does not signal the termination of the parent-child relationship, only an alteration in its format. But the alteration is usually drastic.

In his doctoral dissertation, Fisher (1976) lists six "building blocks" of adjustment to a divorce: (1) self-acceptance: divorce seen not as a personal failure but as a potentially creative reaction to an intolerable relationship; (2) grief or mourning: similar to the process involved in mourning the death of a loved one; (3) disentanglement from the love relationship: the dissipation of one's emotional feelings for the former spouse; (4) rebuilding social relationships: getting involved again in the social world and possibly other relationships; (5) feelings of self-worth: finding new sources of feedback, satisfaction, and a new definition of self other than that of a spouse, wife, or husband; (6) feelings of anger: a natural part of divorcing, which can be positive if used to motivate change, or destructive if used to avoid relationships and responsibilities.

Divorce necessitates change in the marital relationship, in the parent-child relationships, in finances, and in social relationships. No matter how painful it was, the familiar, former life-style breaks apart. In most cases, the custodial parent becomes the primary or only caretaker, and the noncustodial parent finds himself or herself a weekend or occasional parent. Children discover that their relationship with their parents is at least different, in some cases jeopardized. Some children face changing residences, schools, and friends.

There is the loss of usual income and possibly a cutoff of all financial support for one spouse. In 1971, for example, 62 percent of all single parents lived below the poverty level, as compared to twelve percent of all U.S. families. In 1974, nine out of ten single parents were mothers, with a median income of $6,000 (Jauch, 1977).

Changes in social relationships invite dating and introduce the singles scene. Some former friends who are couples drift away. Moving to a new community interrupts previous friendships. The father, who usually is the noncustodial parent, often has to leave the family home and find new living quarters. As a weekend parent, he might feel that he has lost his children as well as his home and his wife. The noncustodial parent faces a less direct influence on child-rearing than was possible before divorce, while the custodial parent frequently has to shoulder more of the daily responsibilities of raising children, although some feel that they were already doing this.

Before changes can be dealt with constructively, before disengagement, self-acceptance and the rebuilding of social relationships can take place, before anger can be dissipated and guilt relieved, the individual must first accept the fact of the divorce and the need for change. This need is signaled by anxiety and insecurity, both normal reactions to significant stress. Anxiety can be faced and mastered, or it can be denied, hidden, blocked, or minimized so that healthy solutions are overlooked.

There are several ways to avoid the truth of one's situation regarding separation and divorce. A first way is through emotional fusion with one's child, so that the child becomes parentified. In this way, the parent lives vicariously through the child, who in turn takes on the burden of caring emotionally for the parent. Although some children will fight this, many accept it ambivalently, since loyalty to the family can be powerful and persuasive. When a parent needs to have a child to take care of, and this relationship interferes with a child's normal development, the parent actually becomes the dependent one.

On an individual level, prolonged depression obscures the changes that need to be made and the feelings that must be acknowledged and worked through. Brief periods of depression are common following a divorce; when they persist they signal that a greater effort needs to be made toward adjusting to the separation and new way of living.

With depression comes helplessness, since the individual gives up actual control over his or her own life. Helplessness prompts more profound depression, thus closing a vicious cycle. Instead of depression, which is amorphous and immobilizing, divorced individuals need to sort out conflicting feelings, including anger, sadness, joy, relief, or grief. Because depression is diffuse, it does not lead to new behavior and adaptation. Being more specific, anger and sadness refer to a certain object, person, or event, and therefore can be worked through more easily.

In place of separating emotionally, while minimizing the need for personal growth and denying the challenge of the new life-style, a spouse can try to change his or her ex-partner. The spouse who is still involved tries to recapture the attention of the disengaged spouse. Dependency on the ex-spouse, or mutual dependency, can be manifested in positive interaction, as when the spouses are overly solicitous of each other and unable to go on alone with their lives. It can also be expressed through ongoing, chronic hostility, in which both are afraid to let go of each other, maintaining their ties by anger. Neither case leads to emotional separation. And when the children are used as a way of maintaining contact, as spies or messengers, the situation is even more complicated and is very likely to be destructive.

By rushing headlong into a new relationship, an individual hides from the emotional growth called for after a divorce or separation. Without greater emotional maturity and an understanding of what went wrong before, sooner or later the same issues emerge in the new relationship. I have frequently counseled a person with multiple marriages, all similar, each one ending in divorce court.

Separation requires time to get one's bearings, to acknowledge, appreciate, and resolve the part the self played in the difficulties of the former relationship. Unless a person has stopped blaming the other and excusing the self, the relationship has not been adequately worked through. Only when an individual accepts responsibility for what he or she did to contribute to the problems are the necessary issues being resolved. For each spouse in a marriage contributed to its failure; each shared in its beginning and in its end.

Integration of the new life-style is under way when the individual accepts the fact of divorce, the need for a new definition of self, changes in the parent-child relationship, and eventually, a rebuilding of social relationships. This changed status comes with intense emotions: anger, sadness, excitement, disorientation, fear. Integration is happening when the individual recognizes both the problems and the promises of the new state in life. A new identity and new direction in life come gradually, only with turmoil, always with anxiety and uncertainty, the by-products of significant change. The freedom of movement inherent in being single (depending on finances and support systems) replaces the togetherness of marriage; the companionship of marriage yields to the aloneness of being divorced. Although some find marriage confining, others discover that being single can mean loneliness.

Finally, there is consolidation.* The new life-style becomes established. No longer a frightening uncertainty, like all of life, it is a mystery to be lived, experienced, and endured. Gradually disengagement from one's former mate takes place; self-esteem returns; the individual again becomes involved with society, new relationships, and self-chosen goals. Blame gives way to self-responsibility; depression and hopelessness to sadness and hope; and bitterness to a calm acceptance of the inevitable limitations of all relationships.

A new type of relatedness with one's child is formed, conditioned by whether one is a custodial, noncustodial, or co-parent. Consolidation has occurred when the spouses are divorced emotionally, but continue as parents, supporting each other as parents despite possible personal antipathy or indifference. Many never achieve this.

CASE STUDY: SUSAN

Susan was twenty-nine, working part-time in a business office when I saw her. Two weeks before the first interview, her husband Frank had left her. A salesman, he had taken a job in another state. Susan and their two daughters were supposed to follow afterwards, once their suburban home was sold. Frank, however, told her that he didn't want them to

---

*A developmental approach to coping with divorce, including the states of orientation, integration, and consolidation is described by Dlugokinski (1977).

come after all. He said he needed "some time," that he was unhappy with Susan and married life. Although there had been turmoil throughout the marriage, Susan was shocked by this. She became depressed, unsure of herself, lost weight, had trouble falling asleep, and blamed herself.

Susan and Frank had been married nine years. Their personalities contrasted sharply. Frank was an outgoing, hard-driving man, always on the lookout for a good deal or a new job. He changed employment frequently, and they moved often. He did not communicate his feelings as a rule. Under stress, he drank, gambled, or used sex for diversion including occasional brief extramarital affairs. According to Susan's description, he gave little of himself personally, although he usually provided adequately for the family.

He left the care of the children to Susan. It was really more her idea to have children in the first place. Although his income was often high, their financial picture fluctuated, due to Frank's proclivities to invest his money in risky business ventures or to gamble.

An only son, Frank was five when his parents separated. His father left and was only marginally involved with Frank afterward. His mother excused Frank's childhood pranks and mischievousness. Evidently, Susan had assumed a similar role in the marriage, covering up for Frank with the children, following after him when he impulsively moved or changed jobs, not raising questions about his use of money or confronting him about his extramarital activities, taking part-time jobs to cover for him financially after he gambled away his pay.

Susan was a quiet, stable, responsible woman, always willing to forgive Frank. She was free with her feelings and often tried to get Frank to open up. She was the oldest of three children in her family of origin: a conservative, Italian-American family. She had always wanted children and did most of the parenting in her nuclear family. Keeping the family together and staying with one's husband were highly prized attitudes in her family of origin and with her.

Susan was attracted to Frank because he was exciting. Whereas she was somewhat constricted in her social attitudes and behavior, Frank was adventuresome, sometimes impulsive, usually stimulating. Together in the early years of marriage they led an exciting, quick-paced, spirited life, traveling, going to parties, moving frequently and spending money. As the marriage went on, Frank gambled, drank more, and began his extramarital relationships. Susan assumed she was the cause and tried to change herself; she became more forgiving, worked harder, took care of the children more, and tried to make herself more sexually appealing. These solutions worked briefly. Overall, the marital relationship varied widely. When it was good, it was filled with adventure and excitement. When it was bad, there was little interaction, closeness, or communication.

Susan did not want Frank to leave, but she had no choice. When he told her not to follow after him, she panicked. She cried and begged him to reconsider.

The separation confronted her with many problems: depression, being a single parent, unsure about what she wanted or how to cope with the separation, what to tell the girls, whether or not to date, what to tell friends and family, but most of all, how to lessen the intense pain and hurt she experienced within herself. She blamed herself and felt guilty.

Through a friend she came to the clinic where I worked. It is not possible to review Susan's entire therapy (Frank was living out of state, and he did not participate), but a broad outline of what happened can be given. Therapy lasted one year. It began as individual counseling and ended as group counseling. Susan learned that her pattern of excusing Frank's irresponsible behavior had not worked. Nor had her acceptance of the major portion of the responsibility for the breakup of the marriage worked (Frank had said that she was no longer sexually satisfying and that is why he left).

Both Susan and Frank contributed to making the marriage what it was and to its outcome: she by her covering up for Frank, which encouraged his irresponsible behavior; he by his irresponsibility, which strengthened Susan's resolve to do whatever was necessary to hold the family together. Who started the pattern was immaterial and unknown. It was the sequence that needed changing.

A self-blamer, Susan became aware that she felt overly responsible for others. A connection with the role she learned in her family of origin was obvious. She had transferred onto her marital relationship her unmet obligations to repay her parents for all they had done for her. To her husband she gave and forgave, excused and overlooked. Frank had been indulged and excused by his mother and probably also felt abandoned by his father. Frank expected, I assumed, that Susan would continue to cover for him and to make up for what he had missed at home. She was a willing partner.

After a few months of separation, Frank panicked and impulsively asked for a reconciliation. Susan had learned by this time that the old way — her overfunctioning* and forgiving and his underfunctioning and impulsive decision making — had been painful and didn't work. She spoke with Frank about what she wanted before a reconciliation could take place: some statement by him that he was willing to explore and work on his part in the marital problems. At one time she would have leapt at the chance to reconcile, but now she knew that this would be more of the same and would probably fail again. Frank wanted things back to the old way. He

---

*For a clarification of overfunctioning and underfunctioning in marital relationships, see Murray Bowen, "Theory in the Practice of Psychotherapy," in P. Guerin (ed.), *Family Therapy: Theory and Practice* (New York: Gardner Press, 1976), p. 80.

tried to induce guilt in Susan to change back. Susan was tested in the ultimate, since feeling responsible for Frank and guilty for the marital problems had been a prime motivating factor throughout their relationship.

Susan resisted the pressure to reconcile impulsively, told Frank what she wanted from him, and waited it out. She knew the risk she was taking—that Frank might file for a divorce, which he did almost immediately. But she also knew that returning to the old pattern of relating was painful, and she decided not to do it.

Perhaps if Frank had been able and willing to seek counseling with Susan, the marital relationship may have been restored. After a while, however, Susan came to the conclusion that Frank's type of man was not what she wanted. She looked for a stable man, who would take more interest in the children and be more affectionate and affirming with her, not one whom she saw as pushing her to be an overfunctioner, a role she was trying to give up.

To what extent Frank was in fact as Susan described is unknown and arguable, since he did not participate in therapy, and I do not know whether he would have participated if he had been available. But even when couples are irreconcilably split, joint counseling is preferable, at least part of the time, so as to aid the therapist and the couple in seeing themselves and each other realistically, without distortion, and to help them disengage constructively.

After considerable turmoil, Susan decided that she wanted more out of life and would only consider a reconciliation if Frank could commit himself to trying to change. Many times she was tempted to go back to her old pattern, but she managed not to. Gradually, the separation became easier to bear.

Besides counseling, other factors helped her make and stick to this decision. I encouraged her to become involved socially, and she went to Parents Without Partners. She started dating, and after several trying experiences, she met a man she liked and who liked her. She utilized the support of her friends, who encouraged her, babysat, and shared with her their experiences with separation and marriage. She got advice from an attorney regarding her financial and legal rights, so that she could maintain a certain amount of financial stability. Her family supported her emotionally and financially.

Counseling was not a cure-all for Susan. The shock and pain of separation wore off slowly. Several times she made progress, only to fall back into depression. But she was willing to try again and always managed to move ahead despite considerable stress and hurt feelings. Selling her large house and moving with her two daughters into a small apartment was particularly difficult. She and the girls both loved the house. More than that, moving represented not only a change of neighborhoods, but it clearly marked a change in the marital and family life. It was a definite break with the past. And a transition of this magnitude always comes with anxiety.

In group therapy Susan learned that many other people faced problems like hers. Their reactions were similar: shock, fear, anxiety, pain, guilt, hurt, lowered self-esteem, depression, and anger. Knowing this helped her immeasurably.

The divorce became final, and Susan stopped therapy. She felt now that the problems that remained could be faced on her own, without further professional help. The symptoms were reduced, not completely eliminated. Susan felt she had the resources to continue without my help or that of group therapy.

This example illustrates the fortuitous interaction of counseling along with the help of various people, including friends, family members, and community and legal resources. Obviously, not all cases work out like this one. Many people do not break old patterns. We were fortunate in this instance not to have any conflict over custody or visitation, which would have been an added strain. But the most important ingredient was Susan's willingness to make use of the various resources available to her.

CASE STUDY: GEORGE

George left Lisa after eleven years of marriage. He said that for five years or more they were in effect emotionally separated although still living together: they communicated little and managed to be apart as much as possible. George was an engineer. On weekends he devoted his time to chores around the house, building and repairing things. Lisa, who refused to participate in therapy, was a part-time accountant. George, thirty-four, and Lisa, thirty-three, had four boys: ages nine, six, five, and two-and-one-half, all living with Lisa. George moved out of the house three months before I saw him. His complaints were depression and guilt feelings regarding Lisa and the children.

He left Lisa with little advance warning. He had been thinking about it for a long time, but their communication was so marginal that he didn't talk to her before leaving. Lisa was bitter, he told me. She did not want George to leave and could not understand why he did.

George related to me that he was the overfunctioner in the marriage, making most decisions, being the one to compromise, making up after an argument. He would drive Lisa places and take care of all household bills and many chores. If she was depressed, he tried to cheer her up. On the surface, he appeared strong and she weak. Yet it became evident in this relationship—as it usually is in overfunctioning-underfunctioning relationships—that George needed someone to rely on him as much as Lisa needed someone to assume control. Mutual dependency was evident.

His leaving was quite out of character and forced Lisa to take care of herself, the home, and the children more. Although she was bright and worked competently as an accountant, at home she was anxious, dependent, fearful, and demanding. The more George did, the less she did. She encouraged him to run the house and make decisions, and the less she did the more George felt it was his job to take care of things. In this process only regressive dependency needs were met; little genuine intimacy occurred. With lines of responsibility being blurred, George assumed responsibility for Lisa's happiness. Having someone rely so totally on him met his need to feel important and useful. George had been growing tired of his role, but he couldn't admit it to himself or discuss it with Lisa. The relationship slowly got worse, and finally George left. It seemed abrupt and uncalled for to Lisa.

Lisa was hurt and vengeful regarding the separation. She told George that he was "rotten" for leaving and that the children should not be exposed to him. Not only did George tell me this, but in a phone conversation with her, she related the same feelings to me.

Lisa blocked visitation: when George would go to see the boys, he was not allowed in the house. The oldest boy would come out of the house and explain that none of them could go with him for one reason or another. Sometimes Lisa would come out of the house and berate George in front of the boys. Previously George had been involved closely with all of his sons. Not only was he now living on his own, but he also had to face being absent from the children in spite of his desire to spend time with them. George felt the boys were being used and were suffering because of the marital dysfunction. Although Lisa seemed to be undermining visitation by discouraging the boys from going with George, he repeatedly would go to the house to explain to her his reasons for leaving, as if she had to accept them for George to be at peace. His attempts at vindicating himself provoked her, just as her opposition to visitation increased his anger. George came to therapy to find a way to lessen his guilt feelings but also to maintain a responsible relationship with the boys.

When I saw George, he felt that he was over the marital relationship, but I was later to find out that he wasn't. Just before leaving Lisa, he began dating Kay. He told me his relationship with Kay was splendid. Almost all that he had hoped for with Lisa was there with Kay. They could talk together and resolve conflicts. They could communicate feelings and show affection.

By the way of background, George was the younger of two children. He had a sister, aged thirty-six. His parents were emotionally divorced throughout most of their married life. Described as quiet and passive except for an occasional violent temper, his father was disengaged from the family, unemotional, bitter about his own life, strict, and authoritarian. George saw his mother as friendly but ineffectual, pleasant but nervous and often depressed. George felt he missed a lot in his childhood and adolescence. He felt his parents let him down because his father was occasionally involved with other women and when that happened, his mother would confide in (parentify) George, telling him her problems, and seeking comfort and advice from him. He listened resentfully.

George had married looking for the ideal close relationship that he still yearned for and for the close, intimate family life he missed as a child. His way of achieving this was to overfunction and overgive, to assume the responsibility for his wife's happiness, and in effect to take care of her as if she were his child. Lisa cooperated.

When the children were born, he felt the need to give them what he himself had missed, as if he were in the place of the children. In other words, he was giving to his children what he had wanted for himself. He was an attentive, perhaps indulgent father. He did not have trouble giving, but he did in setting limits. He was able to be with the children personally, but had difficulties allowing them enough freedom to interact with their peers and other adults. The lack of visitation struck him extremely hard.

The initial thrust of therapy, which lasted twenty-one months, was to take advantage of his desire to be responsible toward his children. If he could find a way to be constructively available to them, he would not violate his responsibilities to them. He would also have to try to disengage from his wife, since he was adamant about ending their relationship. At the same time he needed to examine his part in the marital breakup.

He and I both tried to include Lisa in the counseling. On the phone I explained to her that her participation could help the children adjust. She was too bitter and hurt to come, however. She told me that George was to blame for the situation and refused to cooperate with me. George was "sick," she said; he alone needed help. She could not appreciate that the children would suffer on account of the marital conflicts in which they were implicated. The diminishment of contact with their father and the dispute over visitation, both by-products of the marital problems, would surely hurt them. Lisa felt all problems would be solved if George returned home.

I counseled George on how to approach Lisa about visitation: to make firm "I" statements (Bowen, 1978, pp. 252–54); to avoid being embroiled in bitter exchanges of name-calling with her; to go to court if necessary. Although she eventually consented to brief visitation, later it was necessary to bring the matter to court to obtain a better visitation arrangement. The judge increased visitation somewhat, but this did not remove the children from the throes of their parents' unresolved battles.

George kept up his attempts to be firm and communicate with Lisa — something he found extremely difficult — using the leverage of the court only as a last resort. Lisa gradually became involved with another man. After about nine months, visitation became less contested. After fifteen months, George was seeing the children for overnight weekend visits. Occasionally he saw them during the week.

During the course of counseling, Kay was seen with George at times. The tranquillity of their relationship did not last. It became evident that George had simply jumped from one relationship to another. His tendency to overfunction hid his true feelings: to be outwardly affectionate but inwardly distrusting, and to be highly sensitive to any sign of rejection. These feelings eventually worked their way into his relationship with Kay.

After eighteen months, just before his divorce was to become final, George fell into another depression (he had been free of symptoms for several months) and seriously considered reconciling with Lisa. He did not communicate this to Kay but instead withdrew from her. Eventually she realized that he was going back home a lot more, and she felt George had deceived her.

By spending time with Lisa, George found out that he did not want to reconcile with her. By then, she was not sure she wanted George back either. He attempted to patch up the situation with Kay, but she had been so offended that it was extremely hard for her to try again.

When George stopped therapy he had greatly improved his relationship and visitation schedule with his children: regular, peaceful visitation was taking place. He could also speak with Lisa without necessarily having an argument. He no longer felt guilty regarding the children. He went through with the divorce and achieved some degree of emotional disengagement from Lisa. She apparently had done the same with him. His problems adjusting to his new relationship with Kay were far from settled. But we decided that we had gone as far as we could for now. Gone was his depression, but significant challenges remained.

Summary

Divorce affects every family member. In chapter 5 we saw that divorce causes upheaval in children's lives and threatens their security. In this chapter we discussed how divorce also affects children through the massive life-style changes that press upon their parents.

Families pass through many crises or transitions, but divorce is one of the most serious and stressful changes. Whether it involves disengagement from the former love relationship, coping with anger, guilt, sadness, depression, bitterness, or loneliness, dealing with challenges to self-esteem and self-acceptance, restructuring the parent-child relationship, rebuilding social relationships, or adjusting to moving or reduced finances, divorce demands considerable adjustment.

As a crisis, divorce invites growth or portends disaster. No individual goes through divorce unchanged. Growth depends on the ability to acknowledge the need for change and the strength to patiently work out adjustments. It depends also on the availability of supportive friends and family members, community resources, and helpful organizations.

An individual can choose to confront the exigencies of divorce or to run from them. One can avoid the reality of divorce through overattachment to a child, through depression which blocks constructive actions and drains resources, by trying to make one's spouse different instead of working toward personal change, or by involvement in a new love relationship. All of these turn divorce into a disaster, and none aid adjustment.

Adjustment and growth take time, time to stop blaming and own up to a shared responsibility for the failure of the marriage; time to develop a new understanding of one's self, no longer dependent primarily on feedback from a spouse or children; time to discover that each person has choices regarding new social relationships; time, most importantly, to accept that these demands are difficult and bring with them intense emotions.

With time and effort parents may find that sadness will replace depression, and hope will replace despair; self-responsibility will supplant blaming; emotional disengagement from the former spouse will replace attempts at revenge or reinvolvement; new goals for life will emerge; and an acceptance of the limitations of any relationship will reduce bitterness. When — or if — these changes occur, adjustment is well under way.

By adjusting to divorce, parents not only help themselves but also their children, for adjustment makes coparenting more likely and safeguards the well-being of children. Although certain parents neglect their children on account of selfishness, others are so overwhelmed by the turmoil of divorce that they become physically spent and emotionally depleted. Divorce need not lead to desperate parents or injured children, but it will always be stressful and painful, since anxiety accompanies profound personal change or family restructuring.

Children can cope; parents can help. But this is a topic for a later chapter. Next, the question of who should receive custody will be explored.

SEVEN

Who Should Get Custody?

THE FINAL RESPONSIBILITY for making educational, cultural, religious, recreational, and disciplinary decisions for children constitutes custody. It may include but does not equal physical custody. The custodial parent decides what, if any, church or synagogue a child will attend; what school a child will go to and what curriculum he or she will take up; what leisure activities and cultural pursuits will be encouraged; what limits will be placed on behavior, how those limits will be policed, and what type of discipline and punishment will be meted out if these limits are transgressed; what types of occupations are esteemed; what values are promoted; and what traditions and customs should be observed. The ultimate responsibility of child-rearing rests with the custodial parent, or, in cases of joint custody, with both parents.

Who should be granted custody is, then, an urgent question. The care taken in raising each generation reverberates in subsequent generations. All of society in some way has an interest in custody and visitation determinations and their effects on families. The court, the family, and the clinician, however, have the most immediate concern.

Courts face difficult challenges regarding custody. A judge usually has to decide several cases in one day. The information available to the judge can be meager and superficial, although sometimes it is extensive and thorough. Lacking an ideal solution, or even a good one, a judge is confronted by a conflict of needs and rights. Even though the Uniform Marriage and Divorce Act has called for "the best interests of the child" as the norm for deciding custody and visitation, what these best interests are in fact is vague and hard to discern.

Judges listen to conflicting stories and testimony. Not only do people try to deceive the court, or at least try to present themselves in the most favorable light, but there are also different perceptions of the same event. Meaning varies with the circumstances and the people. When emotions run high, misunderstanding is the order of the day. Even children who clearly express their wishes to a judge may be merely echoing one of their parents' wishes or perceptions. Even if there is enough time, the investigations adequate, and the judge has considerable understanding of the family and its relationships, the final decision often comes down to a choice between two capable parents or two irresponsible ones.

The clinician no less than the judge struggles over custody and visitation. The clinician faces a family caught in the transition of a divorce, undergoing acute anxiety and considerable stress. During custody hearings emotional reactions are intense. Family members tend to blame each other instead of compromising and admitting mistakes. Each spouse wants to see the custody dispute in terms of the other's irresponsibility, neglect, or "sickness," while the clinician looks at it as a family problem, mutually caused and affecting everyone.

The family may want the court or clinician to decide custody, to judge who's right and who's wrong, but the clinician recognizes that ultimately only the parents and children can work out the problem constructively. No court decision can force attitudinal changes or commandeer affection. The court can award custody, but no judicial decree prevents divided loyalties. The court can specify the times and places of visitation, but no judge can stop visitation from deteriorating into a subtle war between parents in which children are the casualties. Nor can a clinician insure what the courts can't.

In an embittered custody battle, each parent is out to win. In contrast, the clinician knows that unless everyone wins to some extent, everyone — especially the children — loses. The clinician speaks to the family not about victory or defeat, but about accountability, responsibility, and mutual parenting, regardless of which parent has legal custody. The family may come for the clinical evaluation to vent hostility, whereas the clinician searches for some common ground upon which to build a compromise. The parents may protest that they are uninvolved with each other, but the clinician sees firsthand that they have failed to disengage emotionally and are in fact profoundly enmeshed.

The reader should keep in mind that I am not referring to families in which there is a minor disagreement about custody or visitation. When the contestation is responsible, when the parents are truly seeking what is best for their children, they are better able to hear that a prolonged and bitter custody dispute will harm their children. They will understand that being responsible means compromise, mutual parenting, and constructive loyalties, not blame, bickering, and divided allegiances.

Custody battles signify that families are entangled with conflicting interests. The dilemma is that the needs and rights of children and parents often conflict with each other. Preoccupied with personal pain, struggling to make sense out of their lives, to decide about their futures, and to build a new life-style, parents may have little time or resources available for their children. Embittered with each other, they are uninterested in forging a mutual compromise. Uncertain about their own futures and insecure about their present circumstances, children have needs and rights of their own. The more children feel neglected or exploited, the greater the demands they place on their parents. Faced with greater pressure, parents become even less available to their children. Unless there are fortuitous circumstances, support from families and friends, professional counseling, or other salutary forces, a negative spiral of disconfirmation sets in.

Parents are trying to salvage something for themselves, a right they certainly have. Buffeted by economic problems and sometimes by social isolation, by a possible loss of self-esteem, by anger, by an unfamiliar life-style, and by an untried autonomy, parents try to be responsible but the pressures in their lives wear them down.

Who Is a Psychological Parent?

Such is the dilemma facing the clinician, the court, and the family. No easy solution can be presented in this book, because none exists in real life. Nevertheless, in disputed custody cases a decision must be made. When parents fail to reach a solution, the court is called upon to decide. As outlined below, courts should favor the so-called psychological parent or parents* in disputed custody cases. (A psychological parent need not be a biological parent.)

The psychological parent or parents may be easy to determine in theory, but it is enormously complex and difficult to decide in practice. The description of what it means to be a psychological parent that follows is of an ideal type, to be used as a guideline. Few if any individuals possess all of the characteristics mentioned. At times, moreover, the decision may be between two mediocre alternatives — or worse — and what is then sought is the least detrimental alternative (Goldstein et al., 1973). At other times, the choice is between two capable (psychological) parents, in which case joint custody, if possible, deserves first consideration.

Psychological parents want custody of their children more

---

*The term "psychological parent" is taken from Joseph Goldstein, Anna Freud, and Albert J. Solnit, *Beyond the Best Interests of the Child* (New York: Free Press, 1973).

for their children's sakes than for their own. Willing and able to care for their children physically and emotionally, psychological parents provide food and shelter and whatever is necessary for the maintenance of life, and give their children a secure emotional environment in which to grow — providing all of these with the least possible disruption to their children's life-styles. Psychological parents do not overindulge their children and thus block their development of competence and autonomy. Nor do psychological parents push their children beyond their ages or resources. They treat their children as children, not as parents or adults.

Psychological parents affirm and value their children for their intrinsic worth, not for earned merit — that is, what children have done or will do for their parents. They love their children more for themselves than for what they can get out of their relationship with them.

Psychological parents possess enough emotional and practical resources to accept parental responsibilities. Any personal problems they might have do not prevent psychological parents from appropriately meeting the needs of their children. If they are depressed, anxious, overwhelmed, angry, hurt, or disillusioned, they are still able to take care of and love their children.

Psychological parents have the courage to be parents even when it hurts. Each psychological parent is committed to the relationship with his or her child despite hardships and pain, financial pressures and loneliness, deprivation, or even rejection. Able to express their feelings openly and constructively, psychological parents encourage their children to do the same, even if these feelings are painful for the parents to hear.

A psychological parent enjoys at least some time alone with his or her child. A psychological parent is willing to do some of the things the child wants, such as playing games or reading stories, and he or she tries to stimulate his or her child to become alert to what is happening in the environment.

Although interested enough to become involved in the lives of their children, psychological parents also have sufficient outside activities and sources of gratification so that their children do not become the focal point of their whole existences.

In a broad sense, psychological parents define their values openly to their children, neither coercing them into acceptance nor permissively depriving them of any reference point or guidance.

Psychological parents take on their legitimate responsibilities for making important decisions that affect the lives of their children and themselves: where to live, whom to befriend, how to budget money, whether or not to separate or reconcile. But they are also able to allow their children increasing freedom commensurate with their ages and capacities.

Of course, psychological parents never ask their children to fight their battles. They never use their children to achieve advantages in the divorce or custody decision.

It is essential for each parent to allow and encourage his or her child's natural loyalties to the other parent and grandparents. The parent who does this fulfills one of the requirements of being a psychological parent; children are spared loyalty conflicts, including the scapegoating or idealizing of either parent.

It is not enough to teach a child what a parent values or to expect adherence to rules; psychological parents also tolerate and affirm differences, allowing their children to develop into first editions, not carbon copies of either parent. Psychological parents teach their values by their living, so that their actions do not make lies out of their words.

Psychological parents see their children realistically; they recognize strengths as well as limitations. No child is scapegoated or idealized. A child is not seen as the embodiment of unacceptable traits that are really within the parent. Nor is the child treated in the image of the ex-spouse.

Reciprocity in relationships — a balance between what is given and received — is taught, encouraged, and lived. Psychological parents, moreover, seek fairness (not necessarily equality) in their dealings with their children. They give generously to their children but also expect some fair return and consideration from them, and they help their children acquire a balance between giving and taking in their relationships with siblings and peers.

Psychological parents admit mistakes but also stand behind what they believe in and what they expect from their children. They do this with calm, loving perseverance. A psychological parent is able to acknowledge what part he or she played in the marital breakup. The feelings a child may have about this, whether anger, sadness, relief, or confusion, are permitted, discussed, and shared. The emphasis is on what the child needs, not on whether the parent likes what he or she hears.

Regarding the separation, a psychological parent tells a child the truth, as appropriate to the child's age, not in exhausting and intimate detail, but as is necessary for the child to understand and work through the separation. It is not that everything is said, but that whatever is said is honest and straightforward.

Psychological parents allow their children to adapt to a separation at their own pace, without imposing their solutions on their children. On the other hand, a parent may share with a child some of the trials and difficulties with which the parent is struggling.

Psychological parents serve as models for their children's development; they teach them how to be men and women, how to pursue a career or make a commitment, and how to invest themselves in freely chosen duties. As models for identification by means of their behavior and not just their words, psychological parents help their children develop a moral conscience or judgment through which concern for the rights and feelings of others is highly regarded, and out of which decisions are made. Values and well-thought-out principles, not whims or vague feeling-states, serve as guidelines.

Because justice is so important and because without a sense of it people go through life trying to make up for previous deprivation, psychological parents do not use their children to advance their own aims: revenge, power, dependency, vindication, mediation, self-esteem, financial advantage, assuaging guilt or reinvolving their mates. Psychological parents are willing to talk with and work with the other parent for their children's benefit, as well as for their own. They understand and believe that the spirit of responsible parenthood is the spirit of cooperation.

Despite pressing personal needs and massive life-style adjustments, a psychological parent is able to remain responsible as a parent. Not as a martyr but as a struggling human being, not perfect but growing, a psychological parent works on personal adjustment and parental accountability jointly, knowing that personal adjustment aids parental responsibility and that parental irresponsibility hinders personal adjustment.

As children age and mature, children should have a voice in who will have custody of them and what visitation schedule will be arranged. They should not have the final say, but their interests and wishes need direct representation in custody and visitation decisions. Children often know which of their parents is genuinely interested in them. If we listen carefully to them, they will tell us. At the same time, some children, out of loyalty, self-preservation, or fear, will express either of their parents' wishes regarding custody instead of their own. In short, children gravitate to a psychological parent, provided they are not being coerced, manipulated, or pressured to favor one parent instead of the other.

SUMMARY

Despite needs of their own, psychological parents are able to marshal sufficient personal resources to take care of their children adequately: to love and want them for themselves; to protect and promote their loyalties to both parents; to treat them fairly and justly; to stimulate them to their environment; to care for them physically, without too much disruption in their style of living; to build trust with them; and to give devotion and make commitments to them. Their relationship with their children is based on reciprocity, a mutual and appropriate giving and taking. No parents meet every criterion listed above. But a psychological parent, whether or not he or she is the biological parent, closely approximates many of them.

EIGHT

Family Therapy During Child Custody Disputes

IN THIS CHAPTER I attempt to outline the approach to therapy that I use with families involved in child custody disputes. The procedures, goals, and interventions of my work are summarized. Two case studies are described.

BACKGROUND

My clinical involvement with child custody and visitation began in 1975 while I was a psychologist on the staff of a community mental health program, technically an outpatient department of a psychiatric hospital (Camden County Health Services Center, Community Mental Health Program in Lakeland, New Jersey). The clinic received a request from the county's Juvenile and Domestic Relations Court to evaluate a family that had been to court repeatedly over visitation conflicts, with no resolution being found. The mother of the four-year-old girl whose visitation was in dispute alleged that the girl was being harmed by visitation with her father. The mother described the girl as having a sleep disturbance, marked anxiety, nightmares, excessive clinging; all of these, according to the mother, were worse following visitation with her father. The parents were separated but not divorced.

119

Another psychologist and I were assigned to do the evaluation. This was the first evaluation either of us had done where the presenting problem was a custody or visitation dispute. We saw the family and sent the recommendations to the court. Although both of us had knowledge and experience in family therapy and other forms of psychotherapy, we were unfamiliar with custody or visitation problems per se and somewhat uneasy about doing the evaluation. This was the first we had seen that had been referred by the court for a custody or visitation evaluation. But it was to be far from the last. The clinic did about one hundred twenty-five of these evaluations a year between 1976 and 1980.

Over the next year, the judge began referring families regularly. The other psychologist and I saw these families as coevaluators and also alone, since we were, at that point, the only staff who had worked directly with this issue. Later, as referrals become routine, most of the staff became involved. From then on I began to learn about custody and visitation problems. They struck me as a variation of other marital and family problems that I had seen. Out of this framework I gradually developed a more formal and systematized understanding and approach to these families. Through collaboration with colleagues, my ideas were fired in the crucible of lively exchanges between staff members.

I decided from the beginning to see the family together. This was consistent with most approaches to family and marital therapy and was my usual procedure for an initial interview of a family with a symptomatic member or one with already identified family problems. It became clear that the nature of custody and visitation disputes made this approach essential. Only if the family took responsibility for resolving the problem was it likely to be settled in a somewhat constructive way. Not unless the family had considerable input into the final decision would it be followed in letter and spirit once the court case was over. Such a resolution, furthermore, could take place only if the family members held a dialogue with each other. A face-to-face interview might initiate this.

Other reasons prevailed on me to see families conjointly. In a divorce and custody dispute, a therapist hears many allegations about both spouses. These allegations are unverifiable unless each party can respond directly to them. A family interview also allows me to see firsthand how family members interact. Finally, I wanted to try to intervene into the way the family relates, not just diagnose or evaluate the family system or the individual members (Musetto, 1978a, 1978b, in press). Diagnosis and pure evaluation encourage the fault-finding and blame that is already rampant in the family. Nor do they help in finding a compromise solution.

Clinical Sessions

I am not the judge of who is right or wrong in a custody and visitation conflict, although I do raise the issue of genuine responsibilities that have been failed or met. Nor do I assign blame, though I explore the accountability of parents to their children and the obligations of children to their parents. I think that a clinician who fails to raise these issues, however painful and complex, does more harm to the family than does the anxiety and resistance that is generated by introducing these topics. And the topics should be raised in a conjoint session with all family members present.

The chief disadvantage of a joint session is, however, that the level of emotions is already so high that a face-to-face encounter might trigger off more anxiety and hostility and serve to underscore the insolubility of the conflict. Another disadvantage is that a family member might be discouraged from revealing certain pertinent information because of the presence of other family members.

Despite the drawbacks, I believe that the advantages of a family interview outweigh the disadvantages. Family sessions emphasize that custody conflicts are family problems, not individual ones, even though each member of the family bears personal responsibility for the origin and resolution of the dispute. A conjoint session stresses family accountability, not individual blame. Seeing the family as a unit makes the point that its members alone carry the responsibility for change: no court or clinician can substitute for parents, and no judge or therapist can enforce decisions in daily living. In addition to family sessions, individual sessions with some or all family members are also important, but this can be done without losing the perspective of custody conflicts as family problems. Yet, individual diagnostic sessions are easier for everyone.

A strictly individual approach encourages parents to avoid a constructive confrontation with each other. Some parents tend to place the responsibility for change in the hands of the clinician, as if the clinician (or the court) will necessarily help the family rather than hurt it. Rather, the clinician's and court's best chance for helping all family members is by summoning them to their responsibilities, enlisting their resources, calling upon their sense of fairness and justice.

Clinicians as well as families will find individual sessions less demanding. Diagnosis is less stressful than intervention. Working with a family is more complex than working with one person, for in a family there are individual dynamics, a system of relationships, and relational ethics to be faced. In short, individual sessions are easier but less helpful.

Several sessions, sometimes three or four are required to reach a compromise, or, in its absence, to make a recommendation to the court. The purpose of the evaluation is to resolve the custody or visitation issue; it is not marital therapy, which could be done later if the spouses request it.

The procedure is for the county Juvenile and Domestic Relations Court, and sometimes the Superior Court, to refer families to the clinic when custody or visitation is disputed. The intake worker of the court advises the family that the entire nuclear family will be interviewed together, that all family members will attend, that a sliding scale fee is charged, that more than one session is usual, and that the purpose is to reduce hostility and conflict among all family members. A letter so stating along with an appointment card is given to the family. Prior to the family coming for the evaluation, I usually receive some information from the court about the family. This may be a brief letter or an evaluation from a lengthy home investigation.

An understanding of the family begins with my first contacts with them. I usually try to observe the family in the waiting room for a few minutes. In the office I look at who talks to whom, who sits next to or far away from whom, whether or not the children spontaneously go to the noncustodial parent, and whether or not that parent responds warmly and easily.

Usually, tension and anxiety pervade the beginning of the first session. It is important, therefore, that I set the tone of the interview from the start, a tone of dialogue, reason, and compromise, marking the session as potentially therapeutic.

Although always subject to variation depending on the particular family, my usual procedure is to give a brief introduction about the purpose of the interview. One ground rule is that everyone will be heard without interruptions. If the family is overwhelmed by anxiety, sometimes I begin by seeing each parent separately and then later bring them together for a family interview.

A family background and intergenerational history on each spouse is taken. I try to avoid the specific custody or visitation issue at first, since this is the issue most likely to lead to arguments and greater anxiety. Getting background information lessens some of the anxiety and also may give me and the family insight into what are some of the unresolved issues that might be blocking a resolution to the current dispute. It also helps the parents and children learn about each other, especially any difficulties the parents may have had in trying to meet their responsibilities as parents. I try to draw out from the beginning that each parent is a mixture of traits and motives, positive and negative, that no one person is entirely responsible for the marital breakup. Ledgers of merit, positive or negative loyalty definitions, a sense of injured justice or one of mutual trust between family members, whether or not exploitation in general and parentification in particular has taken place (Boszormenyi-Nagy and Spark, 1973) — all of these are important to determine as a background to the custody conflict.

A marital history with emphasis on what prevents a resolution to the conflict is reviewed. The custody controversy is usually a continuation of problems that already existed in the marriage and that are exacerbated by the divorce or separation. Underlying motives for the dispute that help to keep the conflict fired up, as described in chapter 5, may come to light, even if the family doesn't explicitly recognize them. Specific feedback loops or problem-maintaining behaviors* (Weakland, 1976) are noted, including pursuit-distance (Fogarty, 1976, p. 326; mind-reading (Grinder and Bandler, 1976, p. 102); induction (Stierlin, 1977, pp. 324–25); family projection process (Bowen, 1976, p. 86); demanding-demanding or oral-dependent relationship (Berman and Lief, 1975, p. 588); overfunctioning-underfunctioning (Bowen, 1976, p. 80); mutual avoidance (neither spouse brings up painful issues); mutual criticism of each spouse's family of origin by the other spouse; catastrophizing (Ellis, 1976, pp. 112–24); rebellion versus excessive rules or abdication of parental responsibilities; contagion of emotion or enmeshment (Minuchin, 1974, pp. 130; 242); anger-anger or mutual blaming.

Individual competences are assayed, but these are secondary to understanding family dynamics and especially to helping the family work out a solution for themselves. I want to

---

*I am indebted to William I. Hopkins, Ph.D., for helping to identify these loops.

understand if there are any factors that might prevent a parent from being granted custody. A history of drug abuse, alcoholism, physical or sexual abuse, psychosis, or previous neglect of the children needs to be carefully examined, but psychopathology is not always a reliable criterion for judging parental fitness. Having already demonstrated responsible parenting is the soundest criterion.

At some point during the interviews, if the family seems interested, I discuss extended counseling for them. Few take this option, however.

A history of the current custody or visitation arrangement is taken. I ask each parent and child to talk about his or her adjustment and feelings about the separation and their custody and visitation situation. I encourage each family member to discuss his or her preference about custody and to listen to and honor the opinions and feelings of the others, even if they disagree with what is said.

The Role of the Clinician

Whereas the preceding section dealt with what goes on in a custody counseling session, this section shows how a clinician can help a family generate its own resolution. In fact, the primary responsibility of a clinician is to facilitate constructive change within the family and only secondarily to evaluate the competence of each parent and the preference of each child.

I believe that the best way to help parents resolve their custody conflicts is by creating an ambience of dialogue and cooperation. Milton Erickson's model of hypnotherapy (Erickson, M., and Rossi E., 1979) serves as a valuable guide. Establishing rapport is the first priority. This is done by building trust, by demonstrating fairness in words and actions, and by instilling the expectation that they will receive help. I listen attentively to them, affirm their right to feel as they do (I could argue with behavior, but not feelings), do not impugn their motivations, emphasize that their struggle for custody reflects on some level their concern for their children, affirm that they ultimately know what is best for their children and themselves and how to achieve it, and underscore that these sessions have helped others and can help them too.

Building rapport merges into depotentiating the usual mindset of each parent and defusing their mutual animosities and avoidances. While the purpose of establishing rapport is to prepare the family to respond favorably to my interventions, the intention of depotentiating and defusing is to set aside the learned limitations and biased framework of each parent — for example, an attitude of blame and revenge — and put a halt to the destructive interaction — accusing and defensiveness, playing one-upmanship, trying to control each other — so that they can use their resources to generate a resolution. The family is asked to stop, listen, and negotiate. Hearing a spouse for the first time can be a revelation, for most people presume that they understand another without really listening.

Finding and explaining positive connotations of each member's behavior (for example, that fighting against a spouse is really fighting to protect the children; that silence is meant to keep the peace) and counterparadoxical prescriptions (for example, since arguing connotes concern for the children and each other, parents should not stop until they find another way to express their concern; in fact the therapist insists that they continue to fight) are especially powerful (Selvini Palazzoli, M.; Boscolo, L., Cecchin, G.; and Prata, G., 1978). In taking a family history, the therapist helps defocus the present animosities and implies that there are explanations for each parent's behavior, however irresponsible it may be or seem. As already stated, breaking destructive feedback loops — for example, blocking parents from accusing each other; raising the relevant issues in front of both parents so they cannot avoid them any longer — also helps in the defusing process.

The family is told that it has the resources to settle its problem. I advise parents that they know how the custody/visitation battle affects their children. Sometimes a firsthand example helps; for instance, when a child looks bewildered and upset in the conjoint interview, I explain to the family that they can see on their children's faces the effects of their controversies. I often ask parents to meet by themselves within the next few weeks and work out a compromise on their own and then return for a follow-up appointment. I tell them that surely they want to decide their own lives, but if they don't compromise, the judge will decide for them.

By bringing to light a common ground of agreement between parents (for example, that both agree that ideally the children should have a mother and father present in their lives regardless of a divorce) and how they have already compromised on certain issues, I capitalize on their resources and build upon them for further compromises. I reaffirm that they know what is best for themselves and their children better than I do — or the judge or their lawyers — and I remind them of their resources, thus trying to activate their inherent capacity to mete out a compromise. If the personal and relationship obstacles can be set aside, if compromise, coparenting, and the best interests of the child can become the objectives, the family will be able to settle the conflict itself.

Finally, if the parents make any steps toward a resolution, I reinforce it, congratulate them, and acknowledge their courage in what they have achieved. If they have resolved the custody or visitation conflict and there are no indications that the resolution would harm the children, I endorse it and advise the court, which allows the family to sign in my presence a consent order that serves as a court order. At other times, a family reaches a partial compromise — for example, agreeing to the fact of visitation — but I have to add to it, perhaps by specifying the times and places for visitation. In those cases that I feel will require the authority of the court and the guidance of a therapist, I advise a follow-up evaluation in six months to one year.

Some families reach no agreement. Then my responsibility is to make a recommendation to the court, that is, to tell them what I believe is the least detrimental alternative available.

CASE STUDY: THE S. FAMILY

The S. family consisted of both parents and two boys, nine and six years old. The husband, twenty-nine, was a carpenter; the wife, twenty-eight, a part-time secretary. After ten years of marriage, punctuated by brief separations, this couple separated for the last and longest time. This occurred nine months prior to the first clinical interview.

Throughout their ten years of marriage, chronic conflict and occasional violence disrupted their relationship. At times, brief separations followed the violence and arguments. A period of relative calm would often be followed by more arguing, thus repeating the cycle. Mrs. S. finally left after she became involved with another man. She and the two boys moved into her parents' home.

Mr. S. was an only son. Both parents being dead, he remembered his father as violent toward him and his mother, a pattern he had partially repeated with his wife, although not as much with his sons. He spoke bitterly about his parents and how determined he had been to have a marriage and family life better than what he had experienced. But his violence was similar to that of his father, and his conflict-ridden relationship modeled his parents' interaction.

Mrs. S. was the younger of two daughters. Her father was described as alcoholic and her mother as intrusive. She lived with both parents. Being told frequently how much her father was responsible for the family's problems conflicted her loyalties. She had sided mostly with her mother against her father. Her husband duplicated her father in terms of his temper and emotional distance, but not in terms of his alcoholism.

The S. marriage began inauspiciously: Mrs. S. was pregnant. She later came to believe this was her exit out of her parents' home. Mr. S. gave little thought to the marriage except that he knew it wouldn't be like what he had witnessed as a boy.

Marital problems surfaced from the beginning. Under stress Mr. S. withdrew into work, hobbies, or sports, away from emotional contact with his wife. When this didn't work, either because it failed to insulate him from his wife or quiet his anxieties, he became violent. As the emotional pursuer (Fogarty, 1976), Mrs. S. was emotionally demanding, verbally the aggressor. Little communication about intimate matters or problems ever occurred. It enraged Mr. S. when Mrs. S. compared him to her father and he would withdraw further.

Both spouses felt they had let their families down by marrying; the stage was set for loyalty to family of origin preventing a commitment to the marital relationship, as described by Boszormenyi-Nagy and Spark (1973, pp. 51–52). They considered it to be fundamental to a successful marriage for each spouse to be able to transfer one's primary loyalty from the family of origin to one's nuclear family. Mr. S. felt he disappointed his father by marrying, since his father wanted him to get established in the family business first. Mrs. S. felt she abandoned her mother by leaving home and failing to provide her with a sounding board for this woman's diatribes against her husband. Mrs. S.'s mother was explicit about discouraging a reconciliation between her daughter and Mr. S.

At the time of the evaluation, the court had temporarily awarded custody to Mrs. S. and weekly visitation to Mr. S., who was allowed to take the children to his own apartment. No problems occurred with visitation until three months prior to the first interview when Mr. and Mrs. S. got into a violent altercation about each other's paramour. After that, the boys allegedly "refused" to see Mr. S. Mrs. S. said, "I will not force them to go if it is against their wishes." But clearly she herself did not want them to go. Mr. S. then filed for custody.

Rancor launched the first interview. Mr. S. accused his wife of neglecting the children, and Mrs. S. said that he upset the children by his hollering. She felt that visitation was harming the children.

The two boys were included in part of the family interview and later seen together without either parent. In the family interview they were quiet and well-behaved. They stayed close to their mother, sitting on either side of her. In the interview without their parents, they were noncommital regarding their parents, except to say that their mother was treating them well and they enjoyed visits with their father. They had stopped going with him because "Daddy is too loud."

My observations and conclusions after the first session were these. The parents were not emotionally divorced, even though both were involved in other relationships. Bitter toward one another, each wanted revenge. Mr. S. was angry that his wife left him for another man. He also wanted to demonstrate to the boys that he, not their mother's boyfriend, was their father, and that he was not abandoning or neglecting them as Mrs. S. was implying. Mrs. S. was angry for the accumulated hurts in the marriage: violence and emotional withdrawal. She was also feeling displaced as a mother by Mr. S.'s girlfriend. She was surreptitiously discouraging visitation as a way of getting back at her husband and controlling their relationship.

The marriage had been replete with conflict and a struggle for control; the custody and visitation arrangements continued this style of interacting. Mrs. S. was discouraged, furthermore, from even considering a reconciliation by intense but subtle family pressure.

A week later, a second session was held with the parents. I

tried several interventions. I reiterated that no one was to blame for the situation, although each spouse contributed to the problem. An ideal solution, I said, was not sought after, only the least detrimental alternative available. I told the couple that we were not meeting to settle their marital problems, but only to decide custody and visitation. Could they marshal their resources so that the children could be taken care of despite the separation and conflict? Scant enthusiasm greeted my comments. More background regarding their families and themselves was taken. At least each listened attentively to the other.

The parents were present for the third session two weeks later. The ambience was calmer and more peaceful; dialogue was beginning. It was as if both spouses had had their say and were now willing to talk realistically about the children. Mr. S. said he had done a lot of thinking. He admitted in front of his wife that he did not really want custody, but he felt that he had to assert his role as the father and demonstrate to his children that he was still concerned. He acknowledged that he had been hurt by his wife and angry with her. He stopped trying to blame her, and she, in turn, lessened her criticisms of him. She remarked that she was learning something about Mr. S. by his admitting what his motives were, and she respected him for this. He was able to say that Mrs. S. was generally a capable mother, with some qualifications. Mrs. S. said she didn't object to visitation and maintained less vigorously that she would not force the children to visit. I reminded her that the boys needed her explicit approval and encouragement or they would probably feel discouraged from visiting and their loyalties would be torn. She said she would think about it.

For whatever reasons, Mr. and Mrs. S. gained enough emotional distance to compromise: she would get custody and he would have regular visitation. Their relationship problems were basically unchanged, but Mr. and Mrs. S. found a way to be more responsible parents in spite of them. They agreed in so many words not to undermine each other as parents.

CASE STUDY: THE Y. FAMILY

The second case example was more difficult, more complex, and more time-consuming. It also had a less favorable outcome.

A twenty-six-year-old husband and a twenty-two-year-old wife had been separated for six months when the first interview was held. After five years of marriage and three children, a boy five years old and twin girls three years old, Mrs. Y. left Mr. Y. because she felt unloved. She complained of little communication with her husband and interference by her in-laws. She moved into her own apartment after the separation, and two months later her boyfriend began living with her. Mr. Y. worked out of state in a semi-skilled occupation and had to move often. He accepted an out-of-state assignment shortly after the separation. His parents (mother forty-five and a father fifty-eight) were taking care of the children. The circumstances surrounding this were complicated.

When Mrs. Y. left, the three children went with her. Essentially, she left while Mr. Y. was at work, giving him no warning. After the separation, Mr. Y. gradually started visitation. During one visit, about four weeks after the separation, Mr. Y. did not return with the children on schedule. Mrs. Y. learned that the children were brought to live with her in-laws, who told her that they would not return the children. She filed for custody the next day.

Despite the court sending the family for the evaluation, Mr. Y. did not attend the first interview because he was out of state, although he had been notified several weeks ahead of time. He left a message that he had been in a slight accident and couldn't make the trip. His parents, Mr. and Mrs. K., attended with the three children. Mrs. Y. was present with her boyfriend. The children and their grandparents, the K.'s, arrived an hour late, without notice. The interview was begun with Mrs. Y. and her boyfriend.

Turmoil surrounded the grandparents' arrival. They walked through the clinic doors hurriedly, speaking loudly, and apologizing for being late, but it was difficult to understand just what had happened. I told them that their son had notified us of his absence. They had also spoken with him.

As soon as she sat down the grandmother claimed that Mrs. Y. was "emotionally unstable": "running around," suicidal, psychotic, and insecure. The grandfather nodded tacit agreement. The battle lines were quickly drawn. By now, I had already spoken with Mrs. Y. and her boyfriend. Mrs. Y., the three children, and Mr. and Mrs. K. were present for the next part of the interview. At my request, the boyfriend stayed in the waiting room. The children went to Mrs. Y. easily and naturally. She was obviously warm and affectionate.

Since the situation was already tense and Mrs. K. had begun to verbally assail Mrs. Y., I interrupted her and began explaining the purpose of the interview. The situation became a little calmer, and I insisted that everyone listen for a moment.

After my usual explanation, Mrs. Y. was given a chance to respond to the accusations, not as in a debate but in an attempt to begin a dialogue and to assert before the others what she wanted to result from the sessions. Her family history had already been taken in the previous hour.

Mrs. Y. claimed that her husband and in-laws were blocking visitation and that they had absconded with the children. Her father-in-law, Mr. K., quickly added that they would not have been forced to do that if she hadn't been so irresponsible and unstable. Mrs. Y. had already told me that she was occasionally depressed and had family problems, but that she felt better recently. Mrs. Y. went on with her response. She said that Mr. Y. had never spoken up for himself in the marriage and that his parents interfered. She wanted custody because she believed she could do an equal and probably better job than her in-laws, but she acknowledged that they were competent and concerned caretakers.

In the interview with Mrs. Y and her boyfriend — to digress for a moment — I learned that she was the youngest of five in a family where considerable family dysfunction was evident. Her mother, described as quiet and reserved, was living close by. The mother had been married and divorced twice. Mrs. Y's natural father was described as violent, a chronic gambler, and absent from home a lot. He and Mrs. Y's mother were divorced when Mrs. Y. was eleven years old. As a girl, Mrs. Y. remembers being anxious, upset, and insecure. Her father would storm out of the house following frequent verbal and physical fights with his wife. Mrs. Y. married at seventeen, yearning for the type of family life she felt she missed growing up.

In the interview Mr. and Mrs. K. spoke for their son, Mr. Y. They said he wanted custody for the children's sake. Considering Mrs. Y. to be unfit, they supported his custody petition, acknowledging that it was really they who would be actually raising the children. Being with them would offer the children more advantages than if Mrs. Y. had custody. The children were already enrolled in school and attended dancing and singing lessons. They also explained that Mrs. Y. was rumored to be about to run off with the children and take them to a cousin's home in another state, so they felt they had to protect the children from this disruption.

The children were seen without their grandparents or mother. Lively, active, bright youngsters, they expressed no preference regarding custody. They liked school, dancing, and singing, but liked their mother, too. They said they did not understand what was happening to them. I observed no particular symptomatology with them.

The K.'s were concerned, bright, and articulate. There was no question about their practical competence in raising children. Married twenty-eight years, they had three other children besides Mr. Y. As Mrs. Y. assured them that she had no intention of taking the children away, the K.'s softened their criticisms. I thought perhaps a dialogue was under way.

Through the insistence of the court, Mr. Y. attended the second session with Mrs. Y. He appeared anxious and unspontaneous. He was angry at Mrs. Y. for leaving, identifying this as evidence of her instability. He felt his parents should have custody given Mrs. Y.'s alleged emotional problems and their superior economic situation (Mrs. Y. was working part-time as a salesperson and her boyfriend was a semi-skilled laborer), and stable home life. He explained that he had wanted the marriage to continue but that Mrs. Y. left him impulsively. Each attempt I made at a compromise or dialogue failed. Mrs. Y. tried to convince Mr. Y. that she had good reasons for leaving, and Mr. Y. wanted her to admit that she was wrong to separate and to acknowledge her overwhelming fault in the marital breakup. Neither compromised.

The third interview, three weeks later, was held with Mrs. Y. and Mr. and Mrs. K. Mr. Y. had gone out of state again. Mrs. Y. had visited the children several times at the K.'s home, and she and Mrs. K. were talking more. The interaction was calmer, less hostile. A compromise seemed imminent. The K.'s felt more at ease knowing that Mrs. Y. was not planning to run away with the children, and Mrs. Y. did not impugn the intentions of her in-laws. All parties agreed to the following compromise: the children would stay with their grandparents, the K.'s, and Mrs. Y. would have regular visitation, including overnight visits every other weekend. As a temporary compromise on both sides, it was understood to be a gradual move toward the children having a chance to be with Mrs. Y. and her boyfriend to determine if they could get along with each other and be adequately taken care of.

The court was notified and agreed to our agreement. A re-evaluation was scheduled in six months. Although this lengthened the time that the children would be in temporary custody, I felt it was necessary because it could lead to a compromise. I was not worried because the children were well cared for on a daily basis. Their individual needs for safety, security, stimulation, and affection were being met by Mr. and Mrs. K. The issue of loyalty and the possibility of them being used as pawns in a power struggle were the problem areas. Futhermore, since Mrs. Y. had acknowledged a previously unstable life-style, it was necessary to see if she could settle down and accept the responsibilities of parenthood before custody could be finalized. There was no serious question in my mind that she wanted the children more for their sakes, as a responsible parent would, than for her own personal advantage. Whether the grandparents wanted the children for their own satisfaction more than for the children's welfare was questionable.

Mr. Y. had the least claim to custody. He seemed least likely to be their psychological parent (since he was least involved with them), was not able practically to assume physical custody (living alone and out of state and moving often because of his job), and, furthermore, he did not really want custody for himself.

Mrs. Y. was uncertain as to how to handle the children, especially in relation to their reaction to her boyfriend. She requested counseling, so I arranged to see her once every two weeks. She acknowledged that the children occasionally acted up with her by screaming, hollering, and being defiant. Her in-laws blamed her boyfriend, but I believed that they were reacting to the pathology of the family system: loyalty conflicts, uncertainty regarding their future, being pawns in a relationship battle, the intense upheaval and anxiety in their lives, possibly different methods of discipline, and the presence of an outsider, Mrs. Y.'s boyfriend, in their lives.

Within a month, I received a call from Mrs. K. who claimed that the children were "unmanageable" after a visitation with Mrs. Y and her boyfriend. She advised me that the children said that they "hated" the boyfriend and that he was "mean." She chided me as to why I didn't do something about it and why I couldn't see what was "really happening." I asked her to come in for a family interview with the children, Mr. K., Mrs. Y., and her boyfriend. She agreed reluctantly.

A few days later I saw the family (Mr. Y. and Mrs. Y.'s boyfriend did not attend). The children's acting out related to an increase in the anxiety and tension that existed between the adults; the boyfriend was an easy scapegoat for this. The uncertainty and disruption of their lives was being felt. The adults' anxiety was contagious, and the children picked it up. Out of loyalty to their grandparents they acted to confirm what was said about them, that they were upset and hard to handle. Apparently, Mr. and Mrs. K. had spoken to their son, who vetoed the visitation arrangement, and I was later to discover that the K.'s were also out to subvert it. I pressed all parties to return again for additional sessions in the interests of the children, but the K.'s failed to keep the next appointment or contact me.

Meanwhile I counseled Mrs. Y. Given the grandparents' resistance regarding counseling, the issue of joint sessions was dropped. Also, in the next session Mrs. Y. explained that the children had calmed down and visitation was smooth.

Mrs. Y. reported a phone conversation with her husband. They argued bitterly; he wanted a reconciliation and she didn't. He supposedly said in anger that she would never get the children back as far as he was concerned. No doubt this had something to do with the apparent attempt by the K.'s to undermine visitation. I asked Mrs. Y. to be in charge of her emotional reactions to Mr. Y, to hold firm to her position calmly, without criticism, and not to withdraw from contact with her husband and his parents.

After three months of visitation, the children were taken on a vacation with their father even though he did not have the court's permission to do this. Angry and upset, Mrs. Y. phoned her attorney, who advised her to wait it out. Meanwhile, I continued to see her.

The date for the six month reevaluation got closer, but the children were not returned to the area. Mrs. Y. couldn't find out from her in-laws exactly where the children lived. By now she had not seen the children for some time. She had spoken again to her husband who was unyielding about not returning the children.

I contacted the court, and it was agreed to schedule the reevaluation in the hopes that the father, children, and grandparents would come. The court wrote to the family giving them the next appointment. On the day of the reevaluation, Mrs. Y. came with her boyfriend, but no one else came. It seemed that she had settled down considerably. By their report (and my observation) she and her boyfriend were getting along well. It was my conclusion that she wanted the children more for their sake, not predominantly for her own. I felt she was capable of meeting their needs. She assured me that she would encourage contact with her husband and his family if she had custody. She felt she could live without custody (it did not seem like she was desperate about it), but she still wanted custody. Her boyfriend said he liked the children and would help support them financially.

After several months of involvement, it was my opinion that the K.'s, although capable in a practical sense, were directly interfering with the loyalties of the children to their mother. They wanted custody as a confirmation of their own self-esteem, with the children being the trophies of their victory over Mrs. Y. Mr. Y. seemed to want custody mostly to revenge his wife, to teach her a lesson, because she left and rejected him.

No compromise was possible. I recommended custody to

the mother and that the court should take whatever action it deemed appropriate to return the children to their mother. (Perhaps some will say that my counseling Mrs. Y. biased me in her favor. But I think that the actions of the various people demonstrated their true motivations and competences. Furthermore, through counseling I could have learned as many damaging things about Mrs. Y. as positive ones.) In fact, I was told that they would try this but that it depended on the cooperation of the court in whose jurisdiction the children lived. Enforcing such an order would be very difficult, unless the children were brought back into the local court's jurisdiction. As of my last inquiry, the children were still with their father.

This complex and involved case is not typical in its length or necessarily in its outcome (one parent absconding with the children), but it does illustrate several features common to most custody or visitation cases with which I have worked or consulted.

One is the conflict of needs and interests between parents and other family members (grandparents in this case) and between parents and children. Each side wanted custody. No compromise was achieved. The needs of the children became secondary to the relationship problems and objectives of some of the adults. Several significant people—the father and grandparents—did not seek out the best situation for the children but instead tried to have custody decided mainly in terms of their own desires.

The custody conflict continued the preexisting marital and family problems. The mother had married in the hopes of achieving the type of family life she felt deprived of, but this was a fraudulent expectation. The father's marital expectations were not clear. Nevertheless, he had grown critically distant and uninvolved with this wife, and she left complaining of his lack of support and his emotional distance. He continued this stance throughout the custody proceeding. His

parents had been, it seemed, overinvolved and intrusive during the marriage and continued to be this way during the
custody evaluation. They pleaded their son's case for custody.
They had de facto custody for some time, without legal claim
to it.

Regardless of what people say, no matter what degree of
concern and altruism is expressed, underlying motives come
to light through patterns of behavior. This is the litmus test of
true motivation in custody or visitation matters (and in most
situations). People are parents by acting as parents, by meeting needs and avoiding exploitation, not by simply saying that
they are parents or giving birth to or fathering children. By
violating the court's regulations and taking the children out of
state, the father and grandparents demonstrated that they
were mostly interested in pressing their own needs, not in
promoting the welfare of the children as the uppermost value.
Their efforts to criticize Mrs. Y. bespoke their intentions to
gain custody for their own purposes. Obtaining custody to
them was not an exercise of responsible caretaking. Although
practically capable and concerned for the children, they
placed their own interests first. Mrs. Y. evidenced mixed motives, too. Although propelled toward custody partially by the
guilt she felt in breaking up the marriage, she showed a willingness to negotiate and compromise, which to me reflected
her deep interest in the well-being of her children.

Custody or visitation disputes usually involve a mixture of
motives. As a clinician, I look for where the balance lies: on
the side of personal interest or on the side of the children's
genuine needs and responsible parenting. I am not pressing
the point that clinicians (or courts) should decide custody;
families should be responsible enough to decide their own
futures, and they should have the freedom to do so. In the
absence of this, however, when the rights of children are
being violated and their needs neglected, clinicians offer a
valuable service for promoting fairness and justice among
family members and helping courts decide custody.

Finally, perhaps the outcome could have been more favorable had I tried to insist on conjoint family therapy with all parties involved. My personal experience has been that mandated counseling is usually ineffective. Other clinicians and other individuals may have different experiences. I believe that it is an open question as to whether or not courts should mandate counseling in cases where it is probable that the children are at a very high risk because of a custody or visitation conflict.

SUMMARY

In working with custody/visitation controversies I have concluded that they are primarily family problems, not the problem of an individual member. Included in my definition of the family are, of course, parents and children, but also grandparents, paramours, brothers and sisters of the children whose custody is contested, aunts and uncles involved in child rearing, extended family members, and significant others. All who are implicated in the problem or who will share in the responsibility of custody or visitation should be involved in the solution.

Because contested custody is a family problem, the counseling and evaluative process, which usually lasts for several sessions, should include at some point a family interview in which all family members are seen together. This emphasizes that contested custody is a family problem requiring a family solution. Although family interviews are anxiety provoking, they provide more reliable information and more leverage to reach a compromise than sessions with only individual family members. Family sessions are not primarily diagnostic; rather, their purpose is to provide an atmosphere in which the family can take responsibility for itself and settle its own conflict.

Clinicians can provide valuable help as parents struggle to resolve custody questions. A clinician's chief responsibility is to create an ambience of dialogue and cooperation, which liberates family members from their attitudinal and relationship limitations so that they can utilize their resources to resolve their problems. The steps to achieving this are building rapport and trust which prepares the family to respond favorably, depotentiating each member's attitudinal strictures and defusing the parents' destructive interacting, reorienting all members toward their innate abilities, capitalizing on their positive motivation and inherent problem-solving skills, and then reinforcing their resolution. In its absence, I make a recommendation to the court about the least detrimental alternative available.

Clinicians do not judge parents; parents by their behavior judge themselves. And the judgment they issue is either one of parental responsibility by virtue of their cooperation, or parental irresponsibility by virtue of their hostility, self-aggrandizement, or power struggles. This judgment comes to light as parents respond to being asked to resolve their custody dispute.

NINE

Children Can Cope, Parents Can Help

DIVORCE IS NOT ALWAYS the worst alternative. Although most children probably prefer their parents to stay together (Reinhard, 1977), some feel relief when their parents separate if the marital relationship has been extremely conflictual. Even in these cases separation and the breakup of the family distress children.

Nevertheless, children can cope with divorce or separation if their parents help. Adjusting to a divorce or separation does not mean an absence of problems or symptoms in children, but that the difficulties are transitory and not generalized to many areas of behavior. Parents should expect some problems with their children on account of divorce and the accompanying massive life-style changes. A bitter divorce and disputed custody multiplies the likelihood of untoward reactions. Whether these reactions will develop into persistent conflicts or be short-lived concerns is discussed in this chapter.

Coping with a divorce or separation depends on the presence of certain key ingredients. Divorce brings with it specific demands and imperatives pertaining to the needs and responsibilities of children and parents. Meeting these imperatives on all levels facilitates adjustment. A prolonged conflict or the absence of one or more of these key elements works against

143

adjustment. These imperatives will be explained below and summarized at the end of the chapter.

ADJUSTMENT IMPERATIVES FOR CHILDREN

For children involved in a divorce or separation the imperatives are: meet their needs, and avoid exploitation.

Repeating from earlier chapters, children require for their psychological development consistent parenting, preferably by both parents. (I am referring to contemporary American society. Whether the same analysis would apply to other societies is open to discussion.) Development in children is encouraged by parents who are sensitive to the effects a divorce has on them without indulging their children's regressive needs. In this sense, parents look for ways to respond positively to their children's behavior without feeding into excessive demands or irresponsibility, such as allowing children to miss school, excusing aggressive behavior, or doing chores for the children that they should do for themselves. Parents help by listening to the hurt their children may experience without shutting them off. They should allow questions that aid children in working through the divorce or separation and the inevitably new life-style that comes with it.

To be loved, wanted, and stimulated, to be physically cared for, to not be scapegoated or idealized, parentified or neglected, to be allowed to retain one's natural loyalties, to be neither overly possessed as the center of a parent's life nor pushed aside as a nuisance, and to be reassured about the future—these are the needs of children during and after a divorce.

When children are assured of a continuous relationship with their parents in the future, they can recall their past experiences with them. When children have no future to look ahead to, the past becomes too painful to recall, because it brings with it a sense of loss. Promising children a future insures both the present and the past for them.

Some symptoms may arise during a separation. Many children become anxious or depressed. Some regress to less mature ways of relating and stop doing things for themselves that they had been doing earlier. They may deny the absence of one parent or the fact of a separation. They become preoccupied with parental reconciliation. Some act out, become irritable or aggressive, or withdraw and seem not to respond at all. Sleeping and eating disturbances, crying, and clinging are common.

Parents should not panic if these symptoms arise; rather, they need to walk a narrow line. They must avoid on the one hand assuming immediately that they have failed and then feel guilty, which often leads to overindulgence and will only reinforce the symptoms. On the other hand, parents should not overlook symptoms that signify that their children feel neglected, that they may want or need more attention, that they feel entangled in the marital relationship, or that significant family problems exist.

Rosen (1977) gives us some evidence that children suffer from marital conflict more than from a separation itself. She studied ninety-two children of divorce, who ranged in age from nine to twenty-eight years old, in Capetown, South Africa. Her conclusion was that an ongoing, unhappy marriage was viewed by children as more difficult to cope with than a divorce. Tension and hostility in a marital relationship disturbed children more than a divorce itself. We might extend this to mean that conflict over custody or visitation augments the difficulties children have in adjusting to a marital and family breakup.

Parents and Families Can Help

Parents themselves face massive readjustments following a separation. One, two, or more years may be needed to make the transition. In these difficult times, parents need financial stability and social supports to be able to help their children cope with the pressures of divorce. Lacking either, their own resources will be strained and their emotional availability to their children lessened.

Parents often react to separation with a bevy of symptoms, including depression, guilt feelings, anger, and insecurity. A sense of helplessness, bitterness, or despair may set in. Shock and uncertainty regarding what to do next and whether they made the right decision siphons their energies away from parental responsibilities.

Parents often question their ability to continue to be parents on account of their personal adjustment problems or relationship difficulties. Can they bracket out their personal problems in their dealings with their children? If parents can look at their children's needs as separate from theirs, whether or not they get along with each other, a milestone is reached. Too often, however, parents subvert themselves by acting out their personal hostilities toward each other through custody or visitation battles. Separating parental responsibilities from marital conflict is as hard to achieve as it is important.

Parents can help their children by allowing them to go through the inevitable anxiety and pain without trying to suppress, deny, or minimize the difficulties involved. Parents help if they allow a genuine expression of feelings, even if they find these feelings painful. Parents do well to remind themselves that they do not have to own their children's feelings: they do not have to be depressed if their children are depressed, angry if their children are angry. They have a choice about how to respond, and their response can be different from the responses of the other people around them.

Parents who strive to be open to questions will allow their children to ask whatever questions they need answered in order to help them make some sense out of what has happened in their lives. On the other hand, parents should avoid making their children confidants regarding intimate personal problems.

Noncustodial parents sometimes say that they are afraid to get close to their children for fear of hurting them. If they are only with their children once a week or twice a month, they wonder if this isn't more painful than not being involved at all and thereby sparing the children the turmoil of coming in and out of their lives. In my opinion, the hurt and pain comes from not having the promise of a future with the parents, more than from their occasional presence. If noncustodial parents can show their children that they will continue to be involved in a significant way, they need not be present all the time; the children will not miss them as much when they leave because there is always more to come.

Nothing substitutes for each parent giving his or her children explicit permission and encouragement to have positive contact and feelings toward the other parent and extended family. This helps preserve the children's intrinsic loyalties.

Despite bitterness or unresolved conflicts, parents can help by not using their children to try to settle their custody or visitation disputes. That is something to be negotiated by parents, taking into account the children's wishes and their own needs. In short, parents should fight their own battles.

Parents facilitate their children's adjustment to divorce by not seeing any of their children as a validation of their own self-worth, personal competence, or parental capability. Parents who fight their own battles without implicating their children in them do not protect the children from any hurt whatsoever, but they provide them with the freedom to work out their reactions without further complications arising from marital troubles. Children cannot really bring back an estranged spouse or rejuvenate a marriage. Parents should communicate directly with each other regarding the divorce and not expect their children to communicate for them.

Parents need to encourage visitation. It is not enough to merely permit visitation in silence. Nor is it sufficient to say, as many parents do, that it is entirely up to the children;

"They make up their own minds," some parents say. In my experience behind this lies an implicit but powerful prohibition against visitation. Active encouragement, explicit permission, and making visitation practical are all necessary. By doing this, parents show their children that they are trying to be responsible even if the noncustodial parent refuses to become involved. Children will be more likely to trust their parents if they show them that contact with the absent parent is encouraged, even if the absent parent did not actually stay involved.

Encouraging visitation and getting along with one's former spouse is also in the custodial parent's best interests. Visitation means time off from single parenthood and allows the custodial parent time to pursue personal goals and leisure activities, or just take a rest from the cares of parenthood. No parent should feel badly about wanting free time. Moreover, a child, in most cases benefits from visitation. Despite what they feel toward their former spouses, parents can press for visitation for the sake of their children. At some point in life a parent may be asked by his or her child why the other parent was not involved more. If the custodial parent has encouraged visitation, he or she can answer the question without guilt.

PARENTS TELL THEIR CHILDREN ABOUT A SEPARATION

I believe that as a rule parents should tell children about an imminent separation and about what is happening regarding custody and visitation. Other writers have expressed a similar view (Gardner, 1976, 1977; Rohrlich et al., 1977; Grollman and Grollman, 1977).

Telling children about an imminent separation serves an important purpose. In spite of parental conflict, the upheaval in family life, new schools or new neighborhoods, the possible absence of one parent, and the appearance of new adults in a child's life, children need to hear and be shown that their parents will work together for them. Both parents talking to the children together is a specific way of meeting some of the child's emotional needs and fulfilling parental accountability. It accomplishes several things.

It reassures children about the future, reducing anxiety and uncertainty. It helps provide for a continuity in parental love and concern. Parents who work together after a separation promote a positive, constructive loyalty within the family; they discourage divided or split loyalties. Telling children about a separation allows them to make some sense out of what is happening to them and their families. It encourages children to own up to, express, and work through their reactions and feelings despite the pain this may cause parents. It demonstrates to the children that their parents are genuinely concerned about the effects a separation will have on them. By speaking honestly and directly to each other, parents and children can be open about what they want from one another during the difficult times ahead.

Speaking to children honestly about divorce, separation, custody, and visitation is a concrete affirmation of trust. By doing this parents declare that they will tell their children the truth, and therefore they can be counted on. They give witness to their being there for the children in spite of the disruption in the family. They also generate hope for the future, asserting that the present difficulties can be overcome. Secretiveness or duplicity, however well-intentioned, make children wary and distrustful, anxious and angry, whereas openness builds trust and assures reliability.

Gardner (1977) recommends that children should be told when a definite decision to separate has been made, one or two weeks before the breakup will take place. According to Gardner, it is important to tell children whatever is needed for a given child to adjust to the separation. The criterion is what the child needs, not what is easy for the parents.

Gardner admonishes not to relate intimate, confidential

information, but the main issues should be aired so that the children understand their circumstances and can be reassured about the future. Parents are warned not to withhold information to protect the image of either parent, because this confuses children, damages trust, and can lead to an unrealistic identification with one parent.

According to Gardner, a child who is old enough to recognize the existence of a parent should be told. Parents who refrain from advising their children about a separation supposedly because the children are "too young" or "too sensitive" are usually rationalizing and trying to allay their own anxieties. Gardner's rule of thumb is: old enough to ask the question is old enough to receive an answer, commensurate with a child's age and sophistication.

Concrete answers should be given. If the father is leaving, the parents should state when and where he's going. If a child is leaving with one parent, he or she should know where they are going. The children should also be told when they will see the other parent, if this is known.

Telling children about a separation requires a free exchange of emotions. Crying by either the parents or the children should not be prohibited, since it is a normal part of working through a separation. Expressing feelings, however painful, is crucial, and parents can model this for their children. It is not that anyone should be overwhelmed by feelings, but only that feelings need to be acknowledged and expressed if they are to be worked through.

Gardner and Rohrlich et al. recommend both parents being present to tell the children. This is a powerful, tangible statement that the parents will continue to act as parents for the children's welfare and not work at cross-purposes. Scapegoating of either parent becomes less likely. Some will argue that seeing parents together encourages children to deny the separation and expect a reconciliation. But if parents provide congruent, clear messages, the likelihood of feeding reconciliation fantasies is reduced.

Parents are advised to give information matter-of-factly, with an ambience of reassurance, encouragement, and hope. Whatever is said should be truthful. If either parent is unwilling to answer a question, that should be said directly. Parents are encouraged to give clear messages and accurate information, so that their children are not confused and do not lose confidence in them.

Language understandable to the children should be used. Parents ought to state directly to their children that questioning is encouraged. Children may repeat questions often because it is their way of desensitizing themselves and adjusting to the separation at their own pace, and they may not understand an answer all at once.

Parents can tell their children about their own mistakes in the marriage. This allows the children to see their parents as human beings, imperfect and struggling to carve out their destinies. It provides an excellent model for the children to identify with. In spite of mistakes, parents should state and demonstrate concretely that they will live up to their obligations as parents. Obviously the children should be told that the separation was the parents' decision, not the fault or responsibility of the children, even if the children were a source of contention or frustration in the marriage.

All of the above presupposes and implies that parents have to be in charge of themselves emotionally and be able to cope with their own anxieties if they are to communicate effectively with their children. Most parents have to be reminded often that they have the resources to accomplish this.

VISITATION

Once custody is decided, visitation must be settled. If joint custody is decided upon, the specific arrangements of it must be worked out. It is extremely important for a child's future development.

The effects of visitation are manifold. Visitation is a practical way of providing children with continued contact with the noncustodial parent and extended family, thus reducing a child's sense of loss. Similarly, it provides the noncustodial parent with a way of being involved and discharging responsibilities toward his or her children. It offers an opportunity for the noncustodial parent to display a visible presence, a presence that will not be exactly the same as before but still one that can be personal and parental. Visitation also helps the noncustodial parent lessen the sense of loss resulting from reduced contact with his or her child.

Contact with the absent parent allows the children to continue identifying with him or her. It also helps preserve the children's natural and constructive loyalties to an absent parent. Visitation permits a wider range of stimulation for the child who may see other adults and children, stay in different places and communities, and be exposed to different cultures and traditions during the course of visiting.

Regular and personal contacts with the noncustodial parent counteract a child's possible feeling of abandonment by that parent. In some cases, visitation, which should be insulated from marital conflict, will provide the noncustodial parent and children with a chance for an even better relationship than was present before the divorce, since the relationship can unfold in a context of lessened marital and family conflict. This assumes of course that the parents are not using visitation to continue their battles with each other.

Visitation should usually be frequent since infrequent visitation tends to make children feel helpless and unloved, and to damage their self-esteem (Kelly and Wallerstein, 1977). Free access to the absent parent is very helpful. Rosen (1977) concluded that this was highly valued by the children interviewed in her study. Free access or unrestricted contact between children and noncustodial parents requires a cooperative relationship between parents.

Rosen lists other types of visitation. One is regulated access, in which there are regularly scheduled visits. This type of visitation may be necessary when marital conflict is still intense and unregulated visitation would be sabotaged by either parent. When a child sees the noncustodial parent sporadically, without a set schedule, Rosen calls it occasional access. This could result because either the child or noncustodial parent is hesitant to have more contact, or on account of the custodial parent's attitude toward visitation, or because of geographical distance. Another form is called no access: all contact between the noncustodial parent and child has ceased. According to Rosen, this usually takes place when the noncustodial parent has forsaken the family. In my experience, it also happens when the custodial parent objects so strongly to visitation that the noncustodial parent becomes discouraged and withdraws from the family.

In Rosen's study, most children (fifty-six out of ninety-two) favored free access. It is her opinion and mine that routine, obligated, duty visits fail to meet a child's needs. Rosen believes that some of the postdivorce problems of children could be reduced by free access to their noncustodial parents.

In her sample forty-eight out of the ninety-two children studied said that the most difficult parental behavior to deal with was the denigration of one parent by the other. In the terminology of this book, the children in these cases face divided or split loyalties.

Rosen concluded that it is not the fact of a divorce but the turbulence associated with it that leads to disturbances in children. This, obviously, is a central idea in the present book.

Kelly and Wallerstein (1977) found that frequent access (two or three times per week), in which children had some sense of control (for example, biking to their father's apartment) helped children cope with divorce. It also helped to reduce feelings of helplessness and lowered self-esteem, often by-products of divorce and separation. In their sample, a five-year research project, two-thirds of the children saw the noncustodial parent twice a month, but most, especially younger children, felt that this was not enough if they and the noncustodial parent wanted to maintain the relationship. Their sample consisted of 131 normal children and adolescents from 60 divorcing families. Those with psychological problems were excluded and referred to appropriate counseling agencies.

Kelly and Wallerstein also found that infrequent visitation, that is, when fathers visited their nine-to-twelve-year-olds erratically, angered these children. The anger in turn discouraged the fathers from visiting and eventually resulted in fewer visits. Probably because they have more capacity to understand a situation and more resources to find alternative sources of gratification, adolescents were less upset by the sporadic schedule. When younger children went for separate visitation their siblings felt cheated unless their fathers devoted time to them also.

Kelly and Wallerstein observed that visitation was increasing and becoming more enjoyable eighteen months after the separation. This suggests to me that as the parents' intense emotional reactions abate—and time itself helps in many cases—children become free to visit more spontaneously. Children with no visitation, 8 percent of their sample, felt "unworthy and unloveable. The seriously diminished self-esteem that eventuates is very difficult to dislodge, even in extensive psychotherapy" (Kelly and Wallerstein, 1977, p. 53).

Kelly and Wallerstein recommend flexible visitation as their chief prescription. Rarely was frequent visitation detrimental in their eyes. Only when the psychopathology of a parent was acted out in the visitation relationship was it advisable to curtail visits. According to them, the presence of even severe individual disturbances in a parent does not necessarily mean that visitation should be restricted. I agree with this, and I have recommended visitation in some cases in which the noncustodial parent had serious personal problems, because I thought that the problems would not be acted out in the parent-child relationship during visitation and that the needs of the children and the potential benefits of visitation outweighed the risks. This is always a difficult decision to reach.

Hope can be gained from Kelly and Wallerstein's study. Even a poor predivorce parent-child relationship does not destine the postdivorce visitation arrangement to failure. The relationship between a child and his or her noncustodial parent can improve after a separation. It seems to be not the fact of a divorce but the divorcing process itself, and how it affects the parents, that shapes what type of visitation if any will follow.

SUMMARY

Although vulnerable and at high risk, children can cope with divorce and its aftermath. Even though they are on tenterhooks, parents can help in this process.

Despite the breakup of the family and custody or visitation conflicts, it is imperative that parents continue to meet their children's needs. These needs include a stable relationship with a loving caretaker, limits and guidance regarding their behavior, being stimulated by their environment, feeling wanted, being encouraged to maintain constructive loyalty to both parents and extended families, and fair treatment. Children need to be spared the exploitation that runs rampant in custody contests; they should not be neglected, parentified, scapegoated, used to fight their parents' battles, or turned into pawns in custody/visitation controversies.

Parents help by being accountable as parents. Accountability comes when parents approach parental responsibility as separate from marital concerns, seek custody primarily for their children's well-being and not as a way of achieving personal gain, and when they encourage positive loyalty and personal contact with the other parent and extended family.

No person, however, is born with accountability; accountability has to be learned, acquired, and fought for.

Children should be told about an impending separation. The imperatives for parents are: be honest and open; collaborate together for the children's good; reassure children about the future; encourage questions; and have a free exchange of feelings and information.

Visitation with the noncustodial parent is a key element in the adjustment of children to a separation. The imperatives for them are: frequent visitation in most cases; free access, with children having some control; cooperation between parents and no competition regarding visitation; and curtailment of visitation only if it is definitely harmful (when a parent's personal problems are acted out in the visitation relationship). Visitation is too important to be entirely in the hands of the custodial parent, although he or she will certainly have considerable input. The fact of visitation should be based on the needs of the children while the specific visitation schedule should take into account the desires of both parents.

Cultural and social factors affect how well parents and children cope with separation. Reflecting on other chapters, the imperatives are: economic stability and the presence of a support system such as concerned friends and relatives, professional or self-help organizations and agencies; cultural attitudes that encourage fathers as well as mothers to be psychological parents and to seek custody; cultural acceptance of divorce and single parenthood as necessary options in certain cases but also cultural attitudes that reinforce the accountability of parents to each other and to their children.

Individual factors affect adjustment. Drawing on previous material, the individual imperatives for parents' coping are: accept the fact of the divorce; acknowledge the need for personal change; identify and work through one's feelings, especially anger and sadness; do not condemn the self or spouse, but learn about the part the self played in the problems; disengage emotionally, not only legally and physically; become involved in social relationships as soon as one is able, but in intimate relationships only after the marriage has been ended emotionally; talk and compromise with one's spouse for the children's and one's own sake; if existentially guilty try to correct the harm that has been done, but if neurotically guilty work through and give up these feelings.

TEN

What Can Be Done

A FAMILY GOING THROUGH a divorce may require professional help. This is even more likely during conflictual and bitter custody or visitation contests that dramatically increase the risk of psychological harm to children. Going for professional help should not be commonplace or undertaken lightly. It is expensive, time-consuming, intimate, personal, anxiety provoking, and intense. This chapter is intended for those families who are considering professional counseling for themselves or for one or more of their members.

WHAT IS THE PROBLEM AND WHO HAS IT?

Problems with custody or visitation reflect a dilemma of conflicting needs and rights, between the parents themselves or between parents and their children. Divorce, furthermore, does not necessarily end the emotional intensity of a marital relationship. Nor does it usually resolve unsettled family issues. Although in time a marital relationship can truly be finished, in a sense parent-child relationships never end. Spouses may change, but parents are parents for life. Even though parenthood is much more than a biological fact, children and parents are inextricably related to each other by blood ties and family loyalty. And these are more powerful forces than are commonly recognized.

The problem is that the family is interacting in such a way that a resolution to the custody or visitation issue is prevented. Interaction imbued with revenge or competition, fights for control or strong dependency ties, bitterness or hostility — all work against a successful resolution to custody and visitation disputes. What is worse, moreover, is when children become inappropriately involved in their parents' personal or relationship problems, as pawns or decision makers, as substitute parents or partners, as scapegoats for the marital problems, as spies or weapons, or as buffers that block communication or interfere with conflict resolution between parents.

Regardless of which family member (or members) shows emotional symptoms, custody or visitation conflicts are family problems. Divorce affects individual family members differently, but every member is affected in some way. The impact a divorce will have on a particular family member depends partially on personality variables, developmental level, previous adjustment, and role or position in the family system. Perhaps even more important than these is the family's inability to cope with the transition of a divorce and the absence of conflict resolution regarding their problems. In short, within the family relationships lies the most important explanation and possible interventions for custody and visitation conflicts.

A particular child can be vulnerable or hurt depending on age, role, personality, and relationship with parents. For example, the marital relationship in a given family places one of the children in the role of go-between. Because of loyalty to the family, the child accepts this position. In some covert way this pleases the parents and gives the child a sense of meaning and importance in life. The specific effect this will have on any child in this situation varies widely. A younger child might feel guilty for the marital discord, an adolescent angry, a school-age child depressed. These are trends discovered through research, but no one can predict for certain what if any symptomatology a given child will have as a result of conflicts about custody or visitation.

WHEN TO SEEK PROFESSIONAL HELP

If custody or visitation is seriously contested and no resolution is worked out, the family should consider a professional counselor. If either or both spouses are uncertain about whether or not to separate, a counselor can help them sort out the alternatives and examine their interaction, with special attention to the specific contribution of each spouse to the disharmony. A multisymptomatic child or a child with symptoms that last for several months is a positive indication for family counseling, especially if the symptoms coincide with the beginning of the separation or if they arise in the post-divorce phase of the family's life. A parent who is unable to adjust to a separation or divorce might require a professional therapist. Another indication for professional help is when both spouses seek a reconciliation but have been unable to bring it about on their own.

Counseling is one option for a family or individual. People should not overlook the support and advice of friends and family or self-help groups, however. Sometimes a combination of counseling and other resources is needed.

WHAT TO DO ABOUT IT

The solution is easy in theory but very difficult in practice. The solution is to work on changing the family relationships in such a way that a resolution to the custody or visitation conflict is found, a resolution that promotes the interests of the children and respects the rights of both parents.

This type of resolution demands the active participation of each family member, especially the parents; each family member must take responsibility for his or her part in producing and maintaining the conflict. The focus is away from detailing the faults and failings of one's spouse or children and towards exploring the part the self plays in the dysfunction. Self-responsibility rather than trying to change the other, dialogue rather than accusations, listening rather than defensiveness, accountability rather than blame, all of these are required. No one person is wholly responsible for the marital breakup. Looking for who is right or wrong discourages taking responsibility for one's self and hides the part the individual plays in blocking a resolution to the problem. When both parents together can attempt to meet their children's legitimate needs, and avoid overprotecting, neglecting, or scapegoating them, a milestone has been reached.

A family in a divorce is a system in crisis. The resulting anxiety tends to provoke dysfunctional behavior: rigid family rules, archaic loyalty demands, hidden alliances or coalitions, excessive expectations, unmet needs, and irresponsible parenting, whether overfunctioning (doing too much for a child) or underfunctioning (doing too little). Anyone who comes into contact with a family in crisis is susceptible to inheriting its anxiety, and anxiety prompts solutions that worsen rather than resolve problems. Extended family members, friends, judges and lawyers, counselors and others are all vulnerable to being affected by intense anxiety that families experience during a divorce or custody controversy.

It is much easier for the court, the clinician, friends, and especially the family to treat individual symptoms instead of family conflicts. It is simpler to work with an individual child whose symptoms may be formidable than to grapple with a complex relational system that has developed hidden rules and loyalties over several generations. It is tempting to see a symptomatic child as the cause of family problems and as a manifestation of individual pathology, but it is really more accurate and more practical to understand a child's symptoms as the result of family relationship conflicts and as a veiled communication about those relationships — more practical because it is more likely to produce an effective and lasting solution, more practical because it is more cognizant of the interdependence of people and society and of the complex nature of human behavior. What is needed is nothing less than a profound shift in horizon: away from simplistic cause-and-effect thinking and towards an appreciation of the interlocking of several levels, the individual-intrapsychic, including developmental level; family interaction and rules; relational ethics (loyalty, justice, fairness, trust); and cultural and social variables.

Further complicating the issue of whether to treat individual symptoms directly or the family system to relieve individual symptoms is the sometimes positive effect of individual therapy with one family member. Bowen (1978) has worked out a method whereby working with one family member can encourage change in the entire family system and each family member. By lessening the anxiety of one member who stays in contact with the family, all members can experience a decrease in tension and anxiety, which will then lead to a reduction of problems throughout the family. Since a family is a system, significant and lasting change in one member can spark changes in other members. Sometimes treating one member treats the system as well.

Another factor regarding who will be treated in therapy is that sometimes all the psychotherapist has to work with is one willing family member. But if the entire nuclear family (and sometimes the family of origin) is available and amenable to counseling, family therapy offers the most comprehensive intervention.

Choosing a Counselor

Selecting an appropriate counselor or therapist may be more difficult than deciding if counseling is indicated. More than one group of skilled professionals offer therapy; these include psychiatrists, clinical social workers, in some states licensed marriage counselors, psychologists, psychiatric nurses, and some members of the clergy. It is my opinion that the discipline of the professional matters much less than the orientation to therapy and the personal qualities of the counselor.

The best recommendation for a therapist is from a satisfied client, someone that the family or individual knows and trusts. Keep in mind that each discipline tends to refer clients to professionals within its same discipline, so that a family physician, for instance, may be more likely to refer someone to a psychiatrist, a medical colleague, than to other professionals. The best referral, however, is one that suits the individual or family, so that the mesh between client and therapist produces positive results.

Families should bear in mind, however, that therapists are not the only ones with responsibility in therapy; the outcome of therapy depends largely on the family. When deciding on a counselor, the family should ask questions and be clear about fees, number and frequency of sessions, missed appointments, previous experience, and orientation to therapy. Will the counselor work with the entire family? Jointly or separately? Will the children be seen? With or without the parents?

A good therapist treats the relevant issues, at the right time, and with finesse. The whole family is part of the problem and should be worked with. As the family relationships change, many of the symptoms in the child will lessen. Sometimes grandparents participate in therapy because whoever is affected by the results of therapy and the outcome of the divorce and custody or visitation arrangements, and whoever contributes to maintaining the problems should be included. To ignore any one of them is to ignore the loyalty and interdependence of families.

Let us review the most important issues for therapy: to help parents move away from preoccupation with simply meeting their own needs and attend to trying to be responsible parents, to put personal problems out of parent-child interaction, and to lay aside interpersonal conflicts in order to coordinate efforts as parents. To accomplish any of these may require a Herculean effort on everyone's part.

Parents also need to work on preserving constructive loyalties. It is advantageous to explore the history of the marriage so that the children will understand what has happened, that no one person was completely responsible for the marriage ending, that the separation was their parents' decision because of marital problems. Counseling for custody or visitation problems is not intended to reconcile parents; rather it is designed to constructively resolve the custody or visitation controversy. Counseling for reconciliation can be done if it is clearly wanted and requested. What is sought after in custody or visitation counseling is the achievement of an emotional disengagement by parents, so that every family member's life can continue unencumbered by further marital discord.

A QUALIFIED COUNSELOR

A qualified counselor has specific personal qualities and clinical skills. Any person who goes to a counselor should feel that the counselor understands his or her unique struggles. A qualified counselor makes the individual feel accepted and understood, not necessarily agreed with. Being a good counselor means to be involved but impartial, fair and objective, trustworthy, free of serious bias, and concerned.

While some individuals are born listeners and skilled counselors, others acquire their expertise by training, education, and experience, all the while building upon their personal assets. These qualifications can be reflected by credentials: by licenses, by graduate degrees, by special recognition of professional societies, by certification, and sometimes by reputation. A clinician skilled and experienced in divorce counseling and the effects of divorce on children is in a favorable position to help. Training and competence in marital and family therapy are prerequisites. A counselor trained and oriented toward individual therapy alone may not be equipped to do couples or family therapy, which requires a thorough understanding of systems and relational variables.

A qualified therapist takes responsibility for the therapy, not for the lives or the decisions of a client. It should be clear to every client what his or her responsibility is and what can be expected from the therapist. The counselor should be responsible enough to attempt to provide a forum conducive to resolving the custody or visitation problem, but the final responsibility for changing falls to the family.

Resistance to Family Counseling

Resistance often greets the idea of family counseling for almost any problem because family counseling means facing difficult issues, and bringing the family together during a divorce or custody determination is especially anxiety provoking.

Resistance arises from several sources. Therapists sometimes resist working with a husband and wife together or including the children in the sessions. Their position on this may grow out of psychoanalytic principles that give primary importance to the patient-therapist relationship without interference from relatives or other family members. Other clinicians may think that a conjoint family session will be too intense and conflictual and therefore damaging to the children. Certainly these sessions are tense and extremely anxiety provoking, but, on the other hand, a resolution is more likely when the entire family is included in treatment. Sabotage by an absent member is reduced. Resistance to change, hidden agendas, archaic loyalty definitions that stand in the way of a resolution, and misunderstandings can come to light. A constructive confrontation among all family members becomes possible. Intervention by the therapist into the family interaction — the recurring patterns of destructive behavior that have their roots in several generations — is also possible, whereas individual treatment focuses mostly on internal states, cognitive processes, and unconscious material, and much is lost by focusing only on these. When families face each other under the guidance of a therapist in an atmosphere of dialogue, ledgers of merit (what one owes the family and what the family owes the individual), loyalty patterns, and feelings of being treated fairly or exploited, surface and can be wrestled with and resolved.

Clinicians do well to remember that no matter how anxiety provoking a conjoint session can be, the children in their daily lives are subject to the conflict and anxiety anyway. Although the family sessions arouse more anxiety than individual sessions, they also engender more hope for a resolution. Some clinicians will oppose my approach for selfish reasons. Traditional diagnostic interviews are lucrative. Those who attempt family evaluations and custody counseling may have to turn down some business on the grounds that their evaluation will only further the contention in the family. It is easy for a clinician to be biased by hearing only one member's account or each member's story separately. If the best interests of a child are really sought, the children and not their parents become the clients. And safeguarding objectivity when a clinician is hired by one parent to evaluate a custody dispute is difficult. Children do not pay fees.

Some lawyers and judges will cast a cold eye on the approach outlined in this book. Adversary in nature, divorce on fault grounds — which requires employing attorneys — embodies the unspoken desire to get as much as one can. This is equivalent to putting the parents' needs and wants above the rights and interests of their children. Some attorneys will be glad of the spirit of cooperation that can grow from custody counseling, but others will believe that they are not doing their job unless they help their clients get as much as possible, regardless of the untoward effects on children. Some attorneys will work cooperatively with clinicians, each struggling to bring about a responsible resolution to disputed custody. But others, fearful of a loss of power and a diminution of their control, will view the clinician as a threat. In each case of contested custody, however, a cooperative relationship between clinician and attorney will aid the family and therefore make the attorney's and judge's tasks easier. No-fault divorce can be a step away from the attitude of defeating one's spouse. But no legal decision, whether it be no-fault divorce or even joint custody, insures parental responsibility and fairness among generations. Only individual family members can do this.

The language of the family-systems approach detailed in this book is that of mutual and reciprocal responsibility, shared contribution to a marital breakup, accountability, compromise, and the ethical dimension of relationships that rests on devotion, commitment, trust, and constructive loyalties. In contrast, the language of the courtroom is often colored by competition and is spoken in terms of blame, fault, and vindication.

More than the clinicians, lawyers, and judges, many families will resist the thrust of this book. Anxiety interferes with an objective appraisal of a situation and brings out rationalization, defensiveness, and selective inattention to unpleasant facts. Faced with anxiety, it is easier to take a child for help than to own up to one's own pain or one's own part in sustaining a problem. Anxiety aggravates rigid family rules that themselves impede conflict-resolution. Rules such as, "Don't discuss painful topics," "Don't compromise," "Don't acknowledge or allow differences in others," "Loyalty to one parent is disloyalty to the other," and others hinder a constructive resolution to conflicts over custody and visitation.

Anxiety can overwhelm family members and block problem-solving. Confronted with the crisis of divorce, family members deny facts, disguise their true feelings, get angry at the wrong person, blame someone else for their failings, pretend to be strong when in fact they are deeply afraid, escape to overactivity, cling excessively to each other, turn to drugs or alcohol to deaden their hurt, seek refuge in superficial relationships, and rush headlong into premature intimacy.

As anxiety mounts, a family becomes symptom-focused. Whatever symptoms a child may have—depression, acting out, irritability, school refusal—commands the full attention of the family, which attempts to relieve these symptoms, thereby avoiding the underlying system and relational problems and each member's contribution to them.

OTHER APPROACHES

There are three other approaches to custody conflicts (similar to what is presented in this book) that the reader should be aware of.

Conciliation Counseling

All families involved in a visitation hearing are referred to the conciliation service (Weiss and Collada, 1977). It differs from my approach in that lawyers are routinely interviewed in order to get their perceptions of their client's needs, to clarify the nature of the counselor's role, and to reduce attorney apprehension and mistrust of the service. The work that I (and my colleagues) have done is mostly for the Juvenile and Domestic Relations Court, where a summary hearing lessens the need for attorneys in many cases. Since there is often a lengthy process of uncovering in Superior Courts, attorneys are a regular part of these proceedings. A substantial number of the families I have worked with did not use attorneys, and those attorneys that were employed were not as involved as they would have been if the cases were heard in the Superior Court. I believe that when attorneys are involved, a clinician should try to work with them and enlist their help for a constructive resolution.

In conciliation counseling, the family, including children of school age or older, are interviewed. The authors report that the initial hostility gives way to counseling that helps resolve the matter in the child's best interests. After counseling, the attorneys are recalled, and the family's agreement is written down and sent to court for the judge's approval. If there is no agreement, the counselor goes to court with an independent recommendation. The authors point out that the focus is on conflict resolution by the parents, not on an imposed solution by the court.

Michigan's Friends of the Court

The purpose of this service is to protect the rights and promote the interests of children. The authors (Benedek, Del Campo, and Benedek, 1977) suggest that "friends of the children" might be a better term. The concept is that of an *amicus curiae*, or the friendly intervention of counsel to remind the court of a legal matter that has escaped its notice and regarding which it appears to be in danger of going wrong. The friend of the court will advise the court of problems, particularly in reference to children, which are not likely to be brought to the court's attention by either parent or the attorneys.

The friend of the court is the director of the department that provides the service. That person is appointed by the governor, upon the recommendation which is usually followed by local circuit judges.

The work of the friend of the court is to investigate all cases involving custody of minor children or child support, and to recommend to the court regarding custody, visitation, and child support. The friend of the court also exercises supervision over all children whose custody, control, or support is determined by the court. Another responsibility is to initiate and carry out proceedings to enforce all support and custody and visitation orders. Friends of the court also conduct hearings when designated by the court to act as "referee" in family law matters, and they petition the court to increase child support, if this is appropriate. Court-connected marriage counseling can be a part of their responsibilities.

Not all functions are exercised equally in practice. Enforcing and collecting child support is the most exercised duty. This is not part of my approach, which is entirely clinical and has no enforcement power.

Mediation Counseling

The purpose of mediation counseling (Druckman and Rhodes, 1977) is for a counselor to serve as a mediator and problem solver to help facilitate the family itself in reaching the best available custody arrangement. What the counselor does is similar to the methods described in this book: he or she clarifies goals, explores alternatives, helps parents negotiate together, and promotes compromises.

A counselor works with the family for six to eight weeks. If no solution is found by then, a traditional custody investigation is made and a recommendation sent to the court. The authors underscore the idea that self-determination is the best way to resolve conflicts, and the family is more likely to follow through on a recommendation if they participate in the decision making. Obviously, I agree with this.

The authors list several advantages to mediation counseling: (1) it lets parents take responsibility for custody and for affirming their love for their child, thus reducing the child's fear of abandonment and guilt regarding the family's dissolution; (2) it reduces a child's vulnerability to court battles; (3) it reduces hostility in a family and therefore the amount of conflict a child is exposed to; (4) it lessens later visitation problems; (5) it decreases litigation in court, because there is less likelihood of reopening custody cases and continuing custody fights.

Summary

Although divorce is painful and bitter custody contests excruciating, something can be done about them. What can be done requires a cooperative effort by lawyers and judges, sometimes by professional counselors, and especially by all family members. A previous way of relating does not bind a family forever; families can change; anger and hostility do not have to dominate its life-style. Although resistant to change, a family can learn to communicate and compromise; it can also learn how to meet each other's needs so that no personal need infringes on the rights of another family member. Whatever it takes to do this—to resolve custody and visitation disputes fairly for all parties—should be done, whether it be through professional counseling, a change in laws or judicial procedures, or different cultural attitudes toward divorce, parenthood, and child-rearing. In this chapter we looked at the contribution of mental health and legal professionals: what they can do, how they can help, and how a family can utilize a counselor's services. Most important, we examined the family's responsibility in settling these problems.

ELEVEN

Special Topics

In this chapter we will examine various proposed legal solutions to contested custody; remarriage as posing specific problems for families and children; certain practical steps a parent can take when trying to be responsible toward his or her children; joint custody, an emerging idea today; and a brief guide for fathers who seek custody.

LEGAL SOLUTIONS

Child Advocate

A child advocate is a *guardian-ad-litem,* someone appointed for the protection of a child during and after a divorce. A child advocate can be somewhat of a surrogate parent, if the parents are so overwhelmed that they cannot meet their children's physical and emotional needs. As of 1977, Wisconsin requires all parents filing for divorce to retain an attorney as guardian-ad-litem, for which the court will pay if the family is indigent (Anderson, 1977).

Family Court

Hebb (1978) discusses the idea of a family court as a possible solution to the many problems of contested custody and visitation. A specially trained judiciary, knowledgeable in the social sciences and expert in divorce and child custody laws, is advocated. Supporting the judiciary would be a pool of various mental health professionals to assist the judiciary in gathering information, interviewing families, and providing short-term counseling. In my opinion these mental health workers should be thoroughly schooled in family and marital therapy so that they understand the complexities of family relationships; they should appreciate the reality and importance of trust, fairness, and constructive loyalty in these relationships.

A family court should be nonadversary, that is, the emphasis should be on mediating among parties, not on conflict, competition, winning, or losing. An informal discussion between parents, which would take place through the family court, might bring out more information than a formal court proceeding. In adversary procedures attorneys are bound by rules of evidence, and both parties try to present a strong argument that may or may not accurately mirror the family situation. This approach often polarizes a family and offers little hope for compromise.

Attorney in Contested Cases

Alexander (1977) has suggested that a committee make a custody or visitation decision. The committee would be made up of specialists, including some of the following: mental health professionals, educators, clergy, and lawyers, plus a trusted adult from outside the family who would represent the child's opinions and preferences.

This proposal raises the question of whether or not a child should have an attorney during a custody or visitation hearing. Does a child have a right to be heard in court and therefore a right to legal counsel? Alexander argues that if a child qualifies as a "person" under the Fourteenth Amendment, then the child has a right to be heard, which implies representation by an attorney.

Alexander lists four options on this question: (1) a child should not have legal counsel; (2) counsel would be appointed at the request of the court or family; (3) an attorney would be required in all cases; (4) an attorney would be required in contested cases and optional in uncontested ones.

Using Alexander's analysis, let us examine each alternative. The first, the quickest and least expensive, rests on the assumption that parents or the state can and should determine what are the best interests of a child. It recognizes that a child cannot make an independent decision regarding custody. The problem with this option is, however, that the parents or the state may not in fact be searching for the child's best interests. As I have stated throughout this work, too frequently parents are promoting their own interests first; and, I would add, sometimes the state or judiciary is unconcerned, uninformed, overextended, and self-serving. (Clinicians are not necessarily exempt from this criticism, either.) Furthermore, a child should have some voice in his or her future and some hearing in court. We cannot assume, consequently, that a child's rights will automatically be protected if the first option is followed.

Although flexible, the second alternative leaves legal representation entirely up to adults' discretion. In contested cases it is highly questionable whether or not parents will act in their children's best interest.

The third alternative is expensive and time-consuming. Adding an attorney increases the complexity of the situation, since another opinion will be heard. In some cases this will increase disagreement and conflict instead of lessening it, although it is hoped that the child will be heard and protected. This option is inflexible because if parents agree about custody and visitation, there may be no need for legal counsel.

Alexander recommends the fourth option on account of its flexibility. Children are most likely to be manipulated or neglected in contested custody cases, when it is most important to affirm their legal rights and protect their interests. Legal representation gives children the same rights as parents; children will be as likely to be heard in courts as their parents. The fourth option emphasizes that the child's needs and interests, not just the parents', are at stake, and these interests dictate what legal safeguards are necessary. Alexander also suggests that because of the stress and conflict inherent in contested cases it is more likely than in other cases that neither parent should have custody. Therefore, it is even more important for the child's rights to be upheld. The fourth alternative, on the other hand, has drawbacks. It is costly and time-consuming and some would argue that it can interfere with parents' rights to privacy. Alexander believes that in uncontested cases there should be a mediator or expert to review the need for legal counsel. Any party—the court, child, parents, or attorney—could request such a review.

I would like to offer the following appraisal and recommendations. First, parents should be allowed to resolve custody disputes on their own. Second, only if they don't should the state, court, or mental health personnel be involved. Third, when any third party is involved, its role should be primarily advisory, to help the family resolve its difficulties with as little interference as possible, but with as much help for them and as many safeguards for the children as are necessary. Fourth, in contested cases, when the family finds no solution, courts will decide the outcome, but they should do so with the assistance of mental health personnel trained in family therapy, including divorce counseling. The judiciary itself should be thoroughly grounded in divorce and child custody laws. Fifth, the resolution should first of all be in the hands of the family because participatory decision making is more likely to be successful; once the court order has been issued and the matter disposed of, the family is left with following it out; it will be more inclined to do so if every member had a voice in the decision. Sixth, although mental health and legal professionals can be extremely valuable, at times indispensable, their presence does not automatically guarantee an outcome that protects the rights and serves the interests of the children without dismissing the needs of parents or violating their legal rights. Sometimes conflict will be so intense that a child will need legal representation and the family clinical intervention. Seventh, it is important to remember that when people make decisions for other people such decisions are likely to be made in the interests of the decision makers and not in the interests of those being decided for.* This should alert lawyers, judges, clinicians, and parents to be on guard lest their services and decisions espouse their own interests and not the interests of those they are serving.

As a specific recommendation, family courts offer much promise. A collaboration of various community resources — legal, educational, and clinical — would be enlisted to help families seek constructive resolutions to contested custody cases. Behavioral scientists and mental health professionals could help train, as well as consult with, the judiciary and its supportive personnel. Marital and family therapists would be available as an option (not mandatory) for couples seeking divorce or differing about custody and visitation. Early intervention can diminish the type of interaction that leads to bitterness and intense conflict, which then puts a stranglehold on the family and endangers the emotional well-being of children. In my recommendation, contested cases would first be sent to family counselors who would work with a family in the hopes of finding a responsible resolution. If none were found, a recommendation (the "least detrimental alternative available") would be forwarded to the court, and at that time an attorney for the child would be enlisted.

---

*Sociologist Marie Augusta Neal (1977) has explained this principle in terms of various minorities and groups with little power.

Although my recommendation in the short run is expensive and time-consuming, I believe in the long run it would prove to be less costly both in terms of psychological problems and in not having to return to court repeatedly for unresolved issues. It requires an availability of qualified counselors, a field that in itself is undergoing scrutiny and criticism today. Naturally, trust between the judiciary and the mental health professions is a prerequisite for it to work.

Finally, I would like to recommend periodic review of certain custody or visitation cases. A review should not discourage the custodial parent from becoming or continuing to be emotionally involved with a child — and it runs the risk of doing this for some people. Nor should it be allowed as a way of continuing a battle between parents. Children need continuity, stability, and secure futures. On the other hand, circumstances and needs change. People grow and change. Children change their minds regarding custody (although it is inadvisable to go to court each time a child expresses a different preference). The emotional stability and life-style of one parent can change so that a child's interests would be served by changing custody (although changing custody, which in itself can be upsetting, has to have a reasonable promise of being better; the good we know now is better than the good we think will come later). Some cases are, furthermore, too complex to be settled all at once; time is needed to test different alternatives. Sometimes time itself lessens the bitterness in a family and therefore allows for a compromise solution in the future, which a premature custody decision could rule out. If parents can resolve the question of custody between themselves, the results will be salutary for their children. Sometimes a temporary order for custody can be made for a specified period (for example, one year) and then reviewed. Certainly, custody should not be changed lightly, and rarely should it be changed at all if a child is already doing well with the present custodial parent. In short, the possible detrimental effects of a temporary order need to be weighted against the potential benefits. But sometimes nothing is lost by waiting.

Like marriage and divorce, remarriage is a transitional or crisis point in a family's life. In 1975, 80 percent of divorced men and women remarried within an average of three years (Thies, 1977).

Remarriage means that a family's nuclear structure changes to become a reconstituted or blended family (Satir, 1972), a family in which one parent is a stepparent. With the loss of one parent and the introduction of a new one, many family issues have to be renegotiated: who has authority, who plays what roles and has what responsibilities, who is included and who excluded, what constitutes acceptable loyalty, and what are the rules regarding affection and emotionality?

Regarding the lines of authority, the custodial parent and the stepparent might define authority and discipline differently from the absent parent, who may see the children regularly and still exert influence over them. Acceptable bedtimes or curfews might vary widely from one household to the next, but children cannot follow two conflicting expectations at once. Unless all the adults communicate with each other and achieve some mutual cooperation, children will be buffeted by confusing norms and conflicting ideals.

Regarding inclusion, the custodial parent and stepparent may act as if those other family members (especially the non-custodial parent) who don't live there don't exist. In fact, however, loyalty ties to a parent can be hidden but strong, and allegiances to absent siblings powerful.

Roles and responsibilities need to be decided based on the requirements of the new family. Small matters can be charged with emotion and conflict: who helps with dinner, who cleans up, who speaks to whom in time of trouble, who lives in what room?

But a definition of constructive loyalty presents perhaps the greatest challenge. Divorce can strain the natural ties that children have to their parents and siblings, usually without breaking them. Unless children have the opportunity to relate to both parents without interference, to decide for themselves what they think about the divorce and remarriage, to have some say about visitation (mostly for older children), the possibility for loyalty conflicts looms great and the emotional cost will be high. Explicit permission and repeated reassurance is needed from both parents to preserve constructive loyalties; tacit approval does not suffice. It is common for a child to have problems relating to a stepparent because of unresolved loyalty to the absent parent. A child needs to feel that it is acceptable to the absent parent to relate positively and to follow the legitimate authority of the stepparent. A stepparent should be aware of the possible difficulties a particular child will have relating well to him or her and allow for this when the child acts out (related to loyalty conflicts). Trust takes time to grow. It comes not from words but from actions. It is built slowly, painstakingly.

Remarriage means an alteration in family relationships. The arrival of a stepparent and possibly stepsiblings reorganizes a family. Since all members of a blended family do not share a common history, it takes time to get to know and respect each other. In blended families where blood ties are not present, the incest taboo is weaker, thereby lessening the built-in restraint on intrafamily sexual relationships.

Remarriage may entail moving into a new home, neighborhood, or state, and changing schools and friends. It may mean a different way of life, a changed financial outlook, or another religious and ethnic background to consider, one with different traditions and norms. Change is usually stressful.

And the changes required by remarriage are no exception.

With remarriage comes the necessity to disengage from the former life-style and grieve for the greater absence of a parent or sibling. Remarriage can touch off or accentuate the feeling of loss a child has for the absent parent. Years may be required for the grief work to be finished. Remarriage presents another danger for parents and children, namely, that remarriage will take place before these issues are adequately worked out. A parent, lonely and carrying the responsibilities of single parenthood, might rush into a new relationship before recognizing the part the self played in ending the previous relationship, and without disengaging emotionally from the former mate. I counseled a woman (along with her husband) who consulted me for marital problems. Her complaint: her present husband drank, and was too passive and emotionally distant. Her previous four husbands had been the same way. Evidently she had not learned sufficiently from her previous relationships to avoid repeating a mistake several times.

Finally, a child must learn how to share the custodial parent with a new spouse, the noncustodial parent with a new mate, and learn how to live with stepsiblings without excessive jealousy and conflict.

The Beleaguered Parent

One premise of this book is that parents, despite a divorce, should work together for their children's welfare. In fact, this often does not happen. I also believe that as parents adjust to divorce, they will be better able to take up parental responsibilities. What happens to the parent who tries to be responsible when the other parent is irresponsible? How can a parent cope with a divorce so as to be in a better position as a parent?

The involved parent faces not only the stress of separation and the demands of adjusting to a new way of life with new interests and goals, not only in all likelihood reduced income, not only a lack of acceptance by some people or a loss of some married friends and perhaps censure by one's own family, but the involved parent may also have to contend with a former mate who is uninterested, irresponsible, or who seems preoccupied with undermining whatever the involved parent tries to do.

Why should a parent try to work things out with a spouse regarding the children after a separation or a divorce? Why should a parent try to compromise with a spouse who is or has been irresponsible, or if there is deep resentment present? Despite a divorce, children need responsible parenting. They are more likely to get what they need if their parents can put aside their hostilities toward each other and work together as parents. One reason, then, to try to work things out is for the children.

A second reason is for the parents themselves. A custodial parent will benefit if his or her children regularly see the other parent; single parenthood is especially difficult without having periodic respites from its daily responsibilities. Visitation or joint custody eases the load. If the noncustodial parent wants to be responsible toward the children and see them regularly, then it is in his or her best interest to negotiate with the other parent. Because he or she has acted responsibly, a parent who has negotiated successfully with the other parent, or who has honestly tried, will be less likely to feel guilty on account of a divorce.

Dealing with one's spouse is a process, not a one-time event. Disagreements and stalemates, strife and anxiety are common. But if parents have the courage to communicate, to keep going with their efforts despite frustration, then they have done something valuable for their children and themselves.

For individuals who feel beleaguered in their attempts to be responsible parents, here are several suggestions.

1. No one should try to change another person; it doesn't work. Even trying to make the person understand a point of view is a subtle way of trying to change him or her. What

works better is to concentrate on the part the self plays in the conflict and then change oneself. Changing oneself invites others to change too. For example, blame fires up conflict; admitting mistakes promotes dialogue.

2. Important principles should not be compromised. A way to assert one's principles while lessening the likelihood of a defensive reaction is to use "I statements" (Bowen, 1978): calmly and uncritically the individual declares what he or she believes and feels, what he or she will or will not do. An "I statement" begins with *I* ("I believe, feel, think, etc."); not with *you* ("You are, should, why don't you, etc."). As an example of what I mean, let us consider the following.

A parent says, "I believe our child should not be asked to carry messages between us," instead of, "Why do you always have to give her the message instead of talking to me?" The tone of the first is assertive. Since the tone of the second is critical, it is more likely to be met by countercriticism. The first is an "I statement," the second a "you statement."

Not only does an "I statement" increase the chances of communication, it also tends to positively influence and have a ripple effect on the other family members. Bowen (1978) has written that if one individual, especially a parent, in a family takes an "I stand," based on well-thought-out principles, sticks to it, and continues to communicate but refuses to feed into the other person's irresponsible behavior, blaming or insults — which no one has to be drawn into — it can have a positive effect on the other family members. It helps them to function better.

3. Each parent should give his or her children explicit approval for them to be loyal and feel positive (if they genuinely can) toward their other parent, even if the other parent doesn't respond. Never should a parent try to get a child to take sides in a marital dispute. Children should see the positive and negative sides of both parents. A parent will be less likely to feel guilty about a divorce if he or she has tried to

encourage the children's loyalty to the other parent and has kept them out of marital battles.

4. With honesty and openness, parents should approach their children about a divorce and custody and visitation, telling the truth at all times. That does not mean that intimate matters need to be detailed, but only that a parent should encourage and answer questions honestly. If a parent is unwilling or believes it is imprudent to answer certain questions, that should be said clearly. Facts such as where and with whom a child should live, how often the other parent will visit (if known), whether the custodial parent will work, who will babysit, what schools the child will attend, and a general synopsis of why the parents are separating, should be discussed with children in a way appropriate to their ages and maturity. Trust builds on honesty, not deception, however well intentioned.

5. Children will experience some pain and turmoil with divorce. Parents cannot protect them completely and should not expect to. Children can see and hear for themselves what is happening. Confusion and distrust result from trying to keep the facts from them. The other extreme is equally harmful — namely, to expect children to solve a parent's problem or shore up a parent emotionally. These are adult responsibilities.

6. Because of the intense stress of a divorce, many children will have some negative reactions (chapter 3). Confronted with a child's symptoms, there is no need to panic. The symptoms will gradually lessen and disappear unless they are mishandled. Panic, overindulgence, or neglect can make them severe problems, instead of passing disturbances. The best way to help a child is for a parent to attend to personal needs (accept the fact of divorce, disengage emotionally from the ex-spouse, work through the separation by acknowledging and resolving intense feelings, rebuild social relationships) and to take up parental responsibilities (meet a child's needs as

best one can, avoid exploitation, keep a child out of marital battles, resolve custody and visitation quickly and fairly for all concerned).

7. The pain of divorce will gradually subside. Involvement with support groups and concerned family members and friends can help. Many people face divorce and survive it. It is not a unique experience, although each person's experience of it differs.

8. To the noncustodial parent: frequent visitation is advisable. If the custodial parent tries to block visitation, be assertive about visitation. As a last resort, after several attempts at dialogue and compromise have failed, take legal action. Children usually do better if they have considerable unhampered contact with both parents, contact that is partially under the child's control. The noncustodial parent ought to be emotionally and physically present and involved.

9. Both spouses contributed to the marital breakup. Trying to figure out which one caused it is not helpful. Trying to understand the part the self played in the conflict is beneficial.

JOINT CUSTODY

Some have hailed joint custody as the best solution to custody disputes in most cases, but an idea that is a revolution away (Roman and Haddad, 1978). These authors stress, as I have already mentioned (chapter 2), that laws and attitudes toward child custody have developed over time. What to some may appear to be an objective fact—that mothers are presumed more fit than fathers regarding custody—came about at least partially for social reasons. Roman and Haddad postulate that women's subordination to men was a crucial fact in the presumption in favor of mothers regarding custody.

Whatever the explanation for this presumption, the point is that if laws have already evolved, they can continue to change today. They are not immutable, simply current practices.

They are matters of fact, not necessity. And, if appropriate, they can be revised again.

Joint custody means that parents will share jointly in the rights and responsibilities of child-rearing. Neither party's rights are superior (Nehls and Morgenbesser, 1980). It does not necessarily refer to joint living arrangements — where a child spends some time living with both parents — although this is often the case. Joint custody has great merit, but it is not a panacea.

Joint custody explicitly recognizes and encourages the involvement of both parents with their children after a divorce. The weight of research that I have cited supports the importance of this. After summarizing research findings, Roman and Haddad reached the same conclusion. (Some, but not all, the research cited in both books is the same.) The accountability of both parents and therefore the greater likelihood that children's trust in their parents will not be eroded, and the easing of daily child-rearing burdens for both spouses speak in favor of joint custody. Moreover, in many cases, both parents are "fit" to have custody, and there is no reason to favor one over the other.

Citing research and other authorities, Nehls and Morgenbesser conclude that joint custody also tends to reduce a child's sense of loss in reference to the noncustodial parent and the noncustodial parent's sense of loss regarding a child. They believe that joint custody has been shown to lessen parental conflict because it eliminates the need for a custody determination — sometimes the most traumatic aspect of divorce — and does not threaten either parent with loss of his or her child. Shared responsibility allows parents, furthermore, to live up to their obligations to their children, thus lessening the risk of parents experiencing destructive guilt feelings.

Notwithstanding its genuine value and current popularity, joint custody has drawbacks. If divorced parents are unable to resolve their conflicts and differences — a frequent occurrence — joint custody provides for an easy continuation of this situation. It may be unreasonable, Nehls and Morgenbesser state, to expect parents to cooperate with each other after a divorce if they didn't while married. Instead of one parent having the final say about important decisions, joint custody can provoke continuing conflict between spouses who have failed to divorce emotionally, *thus leaving the child with no parent, instead of two*. Still caught in the throes of parental conflict, the child is robbed of the opportunity of having the stability and certainty of one parent's authority. Citing Nehls and Morgenbesser again, the increased parental contact on account of joint custody may serve also to deter parents from divorcing emotionally from each other.

My belief is that it does not matter so much what specific custody arrangement is arrived at legally, whether it be joint custody or custody with visitation. Rather, what counts is the mutual cooperation of parents regarding the genuine interests of their children, regardless of the specific legal designation. * What matters is that parents liberate their children from marital problems and that parents meet their children's needs. Each case has to be decided on this basis: what arrangement will come closest to meeting a child's needs. Sometimes joint custody will do this. Sometimes custody with visitation will. Sometimes granting custody to someone other than a biological parent — a person who is a psychological parent — should be preferred. But if two parents, both psychologically capable, can agree and cooperate, joint custody should be the foremost consideration.

FATHERS WHO SEEK CUSTODY

As more fathers seek and obtain custody, the determination of child custody becomes more complicated; there are more options from which to choose.

---

*My thanks to David Cordier, who helped make this idea explicit in my mind.

Cultural attitudes are overturned slowly, however. Many judges still automatically presume that mothers should have custody. Believing that they have little chance of winning a custody petition, some attorneys discourage fathers from filing for custody. The unwritten but widespread presumption that mothers are naturally better suited for raising children deters fathers from seriously considering custody.

Nevertheless, since attitudes are slowly changing, a greater number of fathers will probably seek custody in the future. If they wish to hold their own in court, they need to be prepared to answer a variety of questions about their children. Bernstein, a lawyer, recommends that a father become familiar with his child's needs and activities (1977). He suggests that it is the duty of a lawyer in conjunction with a family counselor to prove to the court who should be the child's custodian. Helping a father learn how to fulfill his child's needs and develop parenting skills is the role of a family counselor.

Although quite capable of being a psychological parent, a father can be unaware of various day-to-day activities and practical details of his child's life. Bernstein advises a father to know the names and phone numbers of his child's pediatrician, dentist, school counselor, and how to obtain emergency medical attention.

A father seeking custody should be able to demonstrate the financial capability to flexibly meet his child's needs. To provide a standard of living that is adequate and approximates the predivorce level is not the sole or most important criterion for deciding custody, but it is one factor and can be influential with the court.

Certainly a father should understand his child's emotional needs and be able to articulate what they are. A father who can give concrete examples of how he has met, is meeting, and will meet his child's needs is in a strong position. Interacting with a child with sensitivity, doing some things that a child wants and enjoys, encouraging positive contact with a child's mother and her family and having a specific plan for achieving this, are excellent ways to demonstrate parental competence.

It is essential for a father to show that he communicates with his child, that he can make himself understood and is able to listen empathetically to the child. A father would do well to be able to answer questions regarding how he would handle minor and major problems or frequent reactions children have when under considerable stress: bed wetting, truancy, school failure, running away, temper tantrums, excessive clinging, nightmares, and expressions of anger.

In essence, an unprepared father will be less able to show the court that he can care for his child. A father who is educated about his child is well-prepared for court; a father who knows his child's physical, emotional, cogitive, educational, and practical needs can present a strong case for custody. All this presupposes, however, that a court will listen and seriously consider a father's custody petition. A court that does not is dominated by unwarranted presumptions and prejudices and is promoting obscurantism in its worst form.

SUMMARY

Children have legal rights just as parents do. How should these rights be upheld? By a child advocate, someone appointed by the court to safeguard a child's rights during and after divorce? By an attorney? In certain or all cases? By a family court, which would use mental health professionals and social scientists to help the judiciary mediate disputed custody? These alternatives were evaluated and recommendations made.

The principles of freedom, caution, and protection ought to guide all child custody decision makers. Freedom means that, above all, families should be allowed to settle their own problems without interference, and only when they fail to do this is judicial or clinical intervention warranted. Those involved in disputed custody as decision makers or advisors should be cautious lest they press their own interests instead of the interests of those they serve. And, finally, throughout contested custody protection of the rights of parents and children should be legally mandated.

In this chapter, I also considered remarriage, which, like divorce, is a crisis or transition that necessitates restructuring of family relationships, including lines of authority and responsibility, inclusion or exclusion of certain members, acceptable forms of intimacy, and, especially, patterns of constructive loyalty. As remarriage results in more blended families, we should pay close attention to the effects on children.

The reader will have misunderstood my intention unless he or she realizes that not all parents seek custody primarily for self-gratification; many struggle to be responsible, often in the face of opposition by the other parent. To such beleaguered parents I offered nine suggestions about how to sustain accountability, and I reminded parents that accountability serves them as well as their children. The suggestions boil down to these: change yourself, not the other parent; hold your ground on important issues; encourage your children to be constructively loyal to the other parent; be truthful to your children about divorce and custody arrangements; let them work through their pain at their pace, remembering that some symptoms are likely; keep going, the sting of divorce will ease; if you are the noncustodial parent, press hard for visitation; forget about blaming your spouse and admit your own errors. Above all, start with the spirit of cooperation; aim high.

Joint custody is a topic on the minds of legislators, judges, and parents, and one likely to be widely discussed in this decade. Joint custody can help insure the presence and availability of both parents, but it can also give them license to continue waging war with one another, thus robbing children of the authority and stability of either parent. Arguments exist for and against joint custody, which should be the foremost consideration when both parents are capable and in agreement — but joint custody is no panacea. I believe, nevertheless, that it will become more popular in the years ahead. The ultimate standard for deciding child custody should still be, however, the best interests of a child, not any particular legal arrangement including joint custody.

Finally, I offered suggestions to fathers who seek custody. Perhaps the day is coming when a father seeking custody will not be unusual.

TWELVE

Toward a Resolution of Child Custody Conflicts

THE PRECEDING ELEVEN chapters attempted to meet several objectives: (1) to understand the dilemma of child custody disputes, that is, the conflict of rights and needs among family members; (2) to provide a practical guide to parents as to how to cope with and resolve child custody controversies; (3) to offer clinicians a theoretical model and some clinical tools for working with families and individuals involved in these controversies; (4) to help courts apply a worthwhile and viable standard for deciding who should have custody and whether or not to allow visitation; (5) to understand the positions children can play in their families when custody is disputed, and what motivates parents to fight bitterly with each other over custody; and (6) to reflect on the reaction of children and parents to divorce and custody problems, as well as to suggest ways to adjust to these difficulties.

DISPUTED CHILD CUSTODY: A DILEMMA OF CONFLICTING NEEDS AND RIGHTS

Of the many transitions or crises families encounter, divorce is a most distressing one. Disputed custody, an outgrowth of unresolved marital and family problems exacerbated by adversary legal proceedings, means that the transition of divorce has not been successfully negotiated.

Court decrees do not dissolve emotional relationships. For some families, marital and family problems continue disguised as custody or visitation contests: the problems that existed in the marriage persist in and promote the battle for custody. Custody contests arise when parents are more concerned with advancing their own interests or in gaining superiority in the marital relationship or divorce settlement than in meeting their children's needs. Parental interests dominating children's needs produce bitter custody disputes that injure children and destroy parental accountability.

In another sense, contested custody is a dilemma of conflicting needs and rights of parents and children. Parents and children both have emotional and practical needs that become more urgent during divorce. Sometimes what children need conflicts with what their parents want or need for themselves.

What are these needs? A secure relationship with at least one caring adult meets a child's needs for safety (physical well-being) and security (building self-esteem and freedom from excessive anxiety). Children also need love, stimulation, affection, guidance, and limits.

Children also need to be treated fairly. Families give to their members — they give life, nurturance, support, knowledge, and socialization — and families expect something in return. A balance between what has been given and received yields a sense of justice, the feeling of having been treated fairly, that an individual may carry throughout life. An imbalance leaves the individual feeling exploited, with a sense of injured justice. Children who are given too much without being able to repay feel indebted, as if they owe their families something. Those given too little feel entitled, as if they themselves are owed something. The former go through life continually trying to justify themselves and overgiving, while the latter demand that others make up for what they have missed. Injured justice violates a child's trust in human relations, trust being the cornerstone of all future psychological development.

Bitter custody contests exploit children. They do this by involving children in their parents' marital battles, by parentifying or holding them unfairly responsible for another family member, by blaming them for the family problems, by depriving them of contact with one or both parents and extended families, and by preventing them from being constructively loyal to both parents.

Children adjust to divorce at their own pace, not at the behest of their parents. They should be encouraged to express and work through whatever feelings they have toward divorce, separation, custody, and visitation, even if these feelings are painful for the parents.

What is also essential for them is to be promised a future in which they will be loved for themselves, not for their achievements, looks, or abilities, or what they can do for their parents.

Parents have needs and rights, too. Stress and anxiety accompany divorce, which disrupts the lives of those it touches. In order to adjust, parents have to disengage from their former mates and to establish a new life-style that includes a rebuilding of social relationships and a changed self-image that takes into account feedback from people other than one's ex-spouse. Parents have to work through their feelings of anger and disappointment, mourn the loss of the former love relationship and end of the marriage, acknowledge the fact of divorce without condemning themselves, and accept the failure of the marriage as a fact of life (something to which each spouse contributed).

The dilemma of child custody and visitation conflicts is that parents' and children's needs and interests frequently clash. Parents can be so overwhelmed by divorce or so preoccupied with their own needs that they are too emotionally depleted to be available to their children. Intent upon gaining some personal advantage or some advantage in their relationship with their former spouses, or wishing to secure an alleged victory in a custody contest, some parents neglect their children, or, at best, put their children's needs second to their own. Like children, parents are vulnerable and emotionally needy throughout divorce and for a time afterwards. During this time they may look to their children to fill the voids in their lives or to meet their needs, instead of taking appropriate care of their children and finding alternative sources of satisfaction in the adult world. Other parents try to be responsible, but conflicts over custody or bitterly contested divorces subvert their efforts. At times, one parent will try to sabotage the other parent's efforts to be responsible. Faced with personal needs and uncertainties, matched by the pressing needs of one's children, a parent may come to feel that he or she has to choose between meeting personal needs (for example, disengaging from the former spouse) and being a responsible parent (that is, encouraging the children's contact with the other parent, which means he or she will have to have contact with that person as well). Such is the dilemma.

THE POSITION OF A CHILD; THE MOTIVATION OF PARENTS

The greatest tragedy of custody conflicts and the greatest exploitation of children occurs when parents use custody, and therefore their children, to try to settle old marital scores, to achieve an advantage in divorce, or to gratify a personal need. Anger converts children into weapons that their parents use against each other. Struggles for control turn children into pawns between their parents. Some parents use their children to assuage guilt feelings about the breakup of the marriage and family, or to lessen anxiety about their new life-style. Parents' dependency exploits children by enlisting them as surrogate parents. Loneliness drives parents to use their children as substitute partners or peers. Parents with low self-esteem expect their children to be trophies, signs of their parental and personal competence. Unable to let go of the marital relationship, some parents pass messages between each other by means of their children, who become go-betweens, while others engage their children as spies. Desperation about family and financial problems pressures parents to expect their children to rescue them by developing symptoms that will re-engage an estranged spouse. A need to blame the other and excuse oneself demands that a child be the judge and jury of parental fault. Lastly, greed relegates children to bargaining chips in divorce negotiations, as if children were personal property to bargain with and about. Several of these roles and motives can exist together.

Since a family is a system, each relationship and individual affects the others; parents need children to play these roles or the circuit will not be completed. Unless a child is willing to spy on one or both of his or her parents, the parents will have to resort to other methods to gain information about each other. Because of loyalty and anxiety about the future, because it gives them some attention, meaning, and importance in life, children accept and sometimes seek out these roles. Children do not assume these roles without parental approval, explicit or implicit. An approving adult and a willing child are both necessary.

Parents Cope with Child Custody Conflicts

Custody disputes are not inevitable; they can be resolved and prevented. Parents can discover that they can defuse their relationship conflicts in order to work together as parents, not spouses, for the welfare of their children. They are divorcing each other, not their children.

Parents can learn not to undermine each other's efforts to be responsible parents. To do this means putting an end to blaming the other person and excusing oneself; as an alternative, a parent should attempt to analyze the part the self plays in the current dispute. Parents must often accept a compromise for the sake of their children, when giving in does not mean giving up, but a declaration that the children's needs come first. It necessitates using justice and fairness in relating to other family members, not revenge and arbitrary self-interest. To achieve this also means talking to one's former spouse calmly and without criticism, taking "I stands," remembering that no individual has to be caught up in another's feelings or irresponsibility; if one parent tries to engage the other in a battle, the second can refuse to be drawn into it. Parents should remember that if one individual takes an "I stand" or makes an "I statement," and sticks to it despite opposition, it tends to have a positive influence, a ripple effect, on the other family members. Talking and compromising are also in the best interests of parents who have enough problems and responsibilities without fighting each other over custody. If the children adjust, the adjustment of parents will be easier. The reverse is also true.

Clinicians Can Help Resolve Custody Disputes

Contested custody is a complex dilemma involving individual, family, relational, and cultural and legal factors. Although each family member, depending on age and role in the family and life-style factors, may develop symptoms in reaction to the stress of a separation and custody dispute, custody and visitation controversies are primarily family problems, not individual ones. They are family problems in the sense that the family relationships block a constructive resolution to who should have custody and whether visitation should be allowed. As an emotional system, an organized group of individuals with patterned ways of interacting, each family is held together by loyalties and bound by family rules. In the interrelationships that make up a family system lie the patterns that gave rise to and sustain a custody or visitation conflict. When they place children's needs second or hinder parents from being responsible to their children, custody disputes violate the trust that should exist between generations. And relationships need trust in order to survive and grow and meet needs. A lack of trust comes from relationships that exploit. There is then another dimension to families, the ethical or relational dimension, where trust or distrust reside, where fairness and reciprocity and justice are found, or, in their absence, exploitation, neglect, and injured justice. Finally, custody and visitation disputes and their outcomes are shaped by laws and cultural attitudes; for example, they may arbitrarily favor one parent, one sex, or one arrangement over another. At the same time, child custody decisions change the laws and reshape cultural attitudes.

As a theoretical framework, clinicians should take into account all four levels and their interaction with each other. The levels are: individual-intrapsychic; family as system; relational or ethical; cultural-legal.

A clinician's chief goal is to help a family marshal its resources to resolve its own problems. A clinician can help do this by asking the right questions: not, who is at fault, but, how does each parent (and family member) contribute to the problem; not, why did this happen; but, what sustains the conflict; not, who should win and who lose; but, how can parents continue to be parents despite their conflicts with each other, and how can both parents function as parents without either being encouraged to abandon a child. The clinician's best leverage is not as an expert with great perspicacity and the wisdom of Solomon, able to decide what's best for other people, but as a facilitator who brings home the point that parents and families help create their problems; that they can change them; that it is in their interest to resolve their problems themselves rather than leave their fate in the hands of a court, lawyer, or clinician; that change requires laying aside blame and making compromises, putting down their weapons and calling a truce; it demands putting children's needs first and self-interest second. It requires, in summary, accepting the principle that the spirit of responsible parenthood is the spirit of cooperation.

A clinician's greatest hope and biggest challenge is to take a family head-on; to see them together as a unit, theoretically and in fact; to deactivate their destructive attitudes and to defuse their harmful ways of interacting; to find their strengths; to build on small compromises; to remind them of their responsibilities; to exhort them to change; and to provide them with an atmosphere in which to cooperate.

Clinicians, lawyers, and judges should cooperate with each other but also be watchful of themselves: making decisions for other people is hazardous. A decision made for someone else is usually in the best interest of those who made the decision. Direct participation by the family in the decision making counteracts this tendency.

Criteria for Deciding Custody/Visitation

In cases where two competent parents cooperate with each other as parents, putting their children's interests first, joint custody (meaning joint decision making and joint responsibility but not necessarily joint living arrangements) is to be preferred.

In all other cases, probably the majority, the criterion of "the least detrimental alternative available"* should be applied. This is because contested custody (which has already followed the crisis of a separation and possibly divorce) injures most children, who are at high risk anyway. Secondly, no guarantee exists that courts or clinicians will arrive at a better solution. In fact, the tragedy may be that no real solu-

---

*The term is from Joseph Goldstein, Anna Freud, and Albert J. Solnit, *Beyond the Best Interests of the Child* (New York: Free Press, 1973).

tion exists; none of the available alternatives may be any better than mediocre. At times, it should be said, there are two fit parents. But to be fit means to put children's needs first, and therefore in these cases a resolution by the family itself is likely.

When parents can't work together in terms of custody or visitation, joint custody seems contraindicated. Joint custody means mutual decision making, compromise, and cooperation. Contested custody means conflict, competition, a lack of compromise. The fact that a custody is contested with any seriousness is already an argument against joint custody for most families. Nevertheless, joint custody helps insure the presence and availability of both parents. It minimizes the sense of loss that children feel regarding their absent parent and that noncustodial parents sense regarding their children, and it affords parents the best opportunity to exercise their accountability as parents. For these reasons, and whenever possible, joint custody demands serious consideration.

If courts are to decide custody, the criterion should be whoever comes closest to being a psychological parent or parents: a person (or persons) who loves and wants the child for the child's sake, not the parent's; someone who has already demonstrated this in fact by a stable, ongoing relationship with the child; someone the child trusts and wants to be with; a person who treats the child fairly, provides limits, guidance, and encourages constructive loyalty to the other parent and grandparents; someone who promises the child a relatively secure future; someone who allows a child to ask questions about divorce, separation, and custody, and to express feelings even if these feelings are painful to the adult. A psychological parent is not necessarily a biological parent, although blood ties and loyalty between family members is pervasive, natural, and enduring and should be preserved first and foremost.

The present standard, "the best interests of the child," is

high-sounding in theory but vague and hard to apply in practice. Nor does it reflect the actual practice of deciding child custody: rarely are the very best interests of children served (or sought), given the intense conflict over custody and the reality that there may be no available solution that will truly promote children's interests.

Visitation is a constructive way to maintaim contact with the noncustodial parent. Research findings support the idea that in most cases liberal visitation ("free access"*) is helpful to a child. Visitation is a good choice unless the visiting parent acts out personal problems directly in the parent-child relationship during visitation or unless it causes a child insurmountable loyalty conflicts. (This applies mostly to young children, is a relatively rare conclusion, and in all cases is very difficult to decide.) As a rule, visitation is too important to be left up to the sole discretion — often, whim — of the custodial parent, although certainly that person would have considerable say in the practical details of visitation; children should have a real voice in it and some control, too. Although at times visitation is fiercely objected to by the custodial parent, the importance of a child maintaining contact with the noncustodial parent usually outweighs the opposition. Unless it is for a very good reason, that opposition harms a child, and it is often a way of revenging the noncustodial parent, who may contribute to the problem by hostility and irresponsibility.

In thinking about custody and visitation, we should remember that the relevant laws and practices are not immutable; they have changed before and are changing now. At one time fathers had an almost unchallengeable claim to custody. Now mothers are highly favored in fact and presumption, if not in theory. Naturally, custody should be decided on the

---

*The term is from Rhona Rosen's "Children of Divorce: What They Feel about Access and Other Aspects of the Divorce Experience," *Journal of Clinical Child Psychology*, 6(2) (1977): 24–30.

basis of the competence and accountability of parents, not on their sex; on the interests of children, not on the unverified prejudices and presumptions of society and its lawmakers.

REACTIONS OF CHILDREN AND PARENTS

At high risk, a risk aggravated by custody and visitation conflicts, children can react to divorce and afterwards with a variety of symptoms: depression, anxiety, regression, acting out, school failure, withdrawal, loss of appetite, sleeping or elimination disturbances, reconciliation preoccupations, guilt feelings, anger, denial, pretending to be brave and unaffected when they really feel afraid and devastated, lowered self-esteem, shame, loneliness — to name some. Not every child is damaged by divorce, but each child is vulnerable at this time.

Research suggests that children at different ages have characteristically different reactions: infants (according to theory and observation, not research) react with sleeping, eating, and elimination disorders; preschoolers tend to feel guilty and personally responsible for divorce, and are without adequate ways to cope; early latency children fear for their futures and the security of their homes; late latency children find themselves angry, ashamed, and lonely, but they actively struggle to master their intense and conflictual feelings; adolescents experience divorce as enormously painful and react with anger, sadness, shame, and feelings of betrayal.

Just as custody and visitation conflicts are not the product of one individual's problems, but are contributed to by each family member, just as these conflicts signify that family relationships are such that no conflict resolution has been found, so also chronic symptoms in children express something about the relationship system (the family) in which they live. They state in disguised form that family problems are present, that needs are not adequately being met, that exploitation may be taking place, that the family as a unit needs help.

Parents can help their children by not overreacting to their symptoms: expect some regression since divorce and its aftermath is highly stressful. Neither should parents overlook genuine problems, however. Parents can prevent temporary hurts from becoming enduring conflicts if they meet their children's needs; keep their children out of their relationship battles; encourage contact with both parents and extended family; promise their children a stable future; insure constructive loyalties; and are emotionally available and involved.

Divorce strikes parents as well as children. Common reactions are: anger, depression, feeling overwhelmed, confusion, lowered self-esteem, guilt, anxiety, loneliness, loss of enthusiasm, self doubts, bitterness, and a sense of failure. To cope with divorce, parents are aided by supportive friends and families and self-help groups (support systems), and financial stability. Sometimes professional counseling is needed to foster adjustment.

CONCLUSION

Perhaps the reader expected a book by a psychologist to be scientific, objective, and value-free. This book is more clinical than scientific; it is based mostly on clinical experience and observation, not scientific research (although research findings are included). That it is objective will be disputed by some. A definite point of view has been put forth, one that no doubt reflects the author's own biases and state of mind. The point of view is that to understand child custody and visitation contests, four levels (and their interaction) should be taken into account: individual-intrapsychic, family as system, relational or ethical, cultural-legal.

Finally, this book is deliberately value laden. The principle values are justice, loyalty, and trust. Justice means meeting children's needs and letting children repay their parents for what they have received; allowing children to be children and not trying to make them into adults; fairness and reciprocity between generations and family members; whereas injustice means using children to try to settle marital problems; seeking custody for some personal or relationship gain; neglecting children's needs in favor of personal desires. Positive loyalty refers to the type of family allegiance that also encourages personal growth and allows for new commitments; whereas negative loyalty occurs when loyalty to one's family conflicts with individual autonomy, or when personal failure is the only acceptable way to show family loyalty. Trust is the confidence in being treated fairly and appropriately now and in the future; whereas a lack of trust denotes an absence of that confidence, a demoralization in general, a distrust of people, and a cynicism about life.

If anyone doubts the importance of these values in families in particular and human relationships in general, let that person examine his or her own experience to confirm or deny what has been said. Has that person never been deeply hurt by injustice; never boiled at being treated unfairly; never wished for revenge when mistreated; never tried to settle accounts with someone; never fought to redress a grievance; never sought reciprocity in relationships; never felt owed or owing? Has that individual never felt an allegiance to a loved one that went beyond purely personal gain or convenience; never been stirred by a commitment to a person, country, or ideal that led to action; never worked hard and sacrificed for a cause, a principle, a value? Has the individual never yearned for someone to trust and be trusted by, someone to count on; never hoped for an honest relationship; never longed for a commitment that would last; never been moved by devotion shown in human relationships?

The presence of these resources — constructive loyalty, trust, justice, and fairness — prevents or resolves child custody disputes. Their absence promotes the type of conflicts delineated throughout this book.

Although I have written at length about injustice, conflict, and bitterness, a current of hope runs through my writing. The hope is based on a belief that people can change. Notwithstanding the personal myths and family roles that deter us, it has been said that people utilize only a small portion of their innate capacities. Perhaps if we draw on all our capacities we can initiate a better future for ourselves and our children.

BIBLIOGRAPHY

Alexander, Sharon J. Protecting the child's rights in custody cases. *The Family Coordinator*, 1977, *26*, 377–382.

Anderson, Hilary. Children of divorce. *Journal of Clinical Child Psychology*, 1977, *6* (2), 41–44.

Benedek, Richard S., Del Campo, Robert L., and Benedek, Elissa P. Michigan's friends of the court: creative programs for children of divorce. *The Family Coordinator*, 1977, *26*, 447–450.

Berman, Ellen M., and Lief, Harold I. Marital therapy from a psychiatric perspective: an overview. *American Journal of Psychiatry*, 1975, *132*, 583–592.

Bernstein, Barton. Lawyer and counselor as an interdisciplinary team: preparing the father for custody. *Journal of Marriage and Family Counseling*, 1977, *3* (3), 29–40.

Bohannan, Paul. The six stations of divorce. In P. Bohannan (ed.), *Divorce and after*. Garden City, N.Y.: Doubleday, 1970.

Boszormenyi-Nagy, Ivan, and Spark, Geraldine M. *Invisible loyalties: reciprocity in intergenerational family therapy*. New York: Harper and Row, 1973.

Bowen, Murray. Theory in the practice of psychotherapy. In P. Guerin (ed.), *Family therapy: theory and practice*. New York: Gardner Press, 1976.

————. *Family theory in clinical practice*. New York: Jason Aronson, 1978.

Buber, Martin. *The knowledge of man*. New York: Harper and Row, 1965.

Carter, Elizabeth, and Orfanidis, Monica McGoldrick, Family therapy with one person and the family therapist's own family. In P. Guerin (ed.), *Family therapy: theory and practice*. New York: Gardner Press, 1976.

Cordier, David. *The effects of pre-therapy training and adjustment to divorce on the outcome of custody and visitation counseling and other related variables*. Doctoral dissertation in preparation, Temple University, 1982.

Derdeyn, Andre P. Child custody contests in historical perspective. *The American Journal of Psychiatry*, 1976, *133*, 1369–1376.

Dlugokinski, Earl. A developmental approach to coping with divorce. *Journal of Clinical Child Psychology*, 1977, 6(2), 27–30.

Druckman, Joan M., and Rhodes, Clifton A. Family impact analysis: application to child custody determination. *The Family Coordinator*, 1977, *26*, 451–458.

Ellis, Albert. *A guide to rational living* (2nd ed.). No. Hollywood, Cal.: Wilshire Book Co., 1976.

Erikson, Erik H. *Childhood and society*. (2nd ed.). New York: W. W. Norton, 1963.

_____. *Identity, youth and crisis*. New York: W. W. Norton, 1968.

Everly, Kathleen. New directions in divorce research. *Journal of Clinical Child Psychology*, 1977, *6* (2), 7–10.

Fisher, Bruce. *Identifying and meeting needs of formerly married people through a divorce adjustment seminar*. Unpublished doctoral dissertation, University of Northern Colorado, 1976.

Fogarty, Thomas F. Marital crisis. In P. Guerin (ed.), *Family therapy: theory and practice*. New York: Gardner Press, 1976.

Gardner, Richard A. *Psychotherapy with children of divorce*. New York: Jason Aronson, 1976.

_____. Children of divorce: some legal and psychological considerations. *Journal of Clinical Child Psychology*, 1977, *6* (2), p. 3–6.

Goldman, Janice and Coane, James. Family therapy after the divorce: developing a strategy. *Family Process*, 1977, *16*, 357–362.

Goldstein, Joseph, Freud, Anna, and Solnit, Albert J. *Beyond the best interests of the child*. New York: Free Press, 1973.

Grinder, John, and Bandler, Richard. *The structure of magic* (Vol. 2). Palo Alto, Cal.: Science and Behavior Books, 1976.

Grollman, Earl A., and Grollman, Sharon H. How to tell children about divorce. *Journal of Clinical Child Psychology*, 1977, *6* (2), 35–37.

Guerin, Philip J. Jr. Family therapy: the first twenty-five years. In P. Guerin (ed.), *Family therapy: theory and practice*. New York: Gardner Press, 1976.

Haley, Jay. *Strategies of psychotherapy*. New York: Grune and Stratton, 1963.

Hebb, Dorcas. *Life without father: child custody in Maine*. Unpublished manuscript, 1978. (Report prepared for the Maine Civil Liberties Union).

Henning, James S., and Oldham, J. Thomas. Children of divorce: legal and psychological crises. *Journal of Clinical Child Psychology*, 1977, *6* (2), 55–58.

Jauch, Carol. The one-parent family. *Journal of Clinical Child Psychology*, 1977, *6* (2), 30–32.

Kelly, Joan B., and Wallerstein, Judith S. Part-time parent, part-time child: visiting after divorce. *Journal of Clinical Child Psychology*, 1977, *6* (2), 51–54.

Kohlberg, Lawrence. The development of children's orientation toward a moral order. 1. Sequence in the development of moral thought. *Vita Humana*, 1963, *6*, 11–33.

_____. Moral development. *In International encyclopedia of the social sciences* (Vol. 10). New York: Free Press, 1968.

Laing, R. D. *The politics of the family and other essays*. New York: Vintage Publications, 1972.

Minuchin, Salvador. *Families and family therapy.* Cambridge, Mass.: Harvard University Press, 1974.

Musetto, Andrew P. Evaluating families with custody or visitation problems. *Journal of Marriage and Family Counseling,* 1978a, *4* (4), 59–65.

_____. Child custody and visitation: the role of the clinician in relation to the family. *Family Therapy,* 1978b, 5, 143–150.

_____. The role of the mental health professional in contested custody: Evaluator of competence or facilitator of change. *Journal of Divorce.* In press.

National Conference of Commissioners on Uniform State Laws. *Uniform marriage and divorce act.* Chicago, Ill., 1970. (Amended, 1971 and 1973).

Nehls, Nadine, and Morgenbesser, Mel. Joint custody: An exploration of the issues. *Family Process,* 1980, *19* (2), 117–25.

Parks, Ann. Children and youth of divorce in Parents Without Partners, Inc. *Journal of Clinical Child Psychology,* 1977, *6* (2), 44–48.

Piaget, Jean. *The moral judgement of the child.* New York: Free Press, 1965.

Reinhard, David W. The reaction of adolescent boys and girls to the divorce of their parents. *Journal of Clinical Child Psychology,* 1977, *6* (2), 21–23.

Rohrlich, John A., Ranier, Ruth, Berg-Cross, Linda, and Berg-Cross, Gary. The effects of divorce: a research review with a developmental perspective. *Journal of Clinical Child Psychology,* 1977, *6* (2), 15–20.

Roman, Mel, and Haddad, William. *The disposable parent: the case for joint custody.* New York: Holt, Rinehart and Winston, 1978.

Rosen, Rhona. Children of divorce: what they feel about access and other aspects of the divorce experience. *Journal of Clinical Child Psychology,* 1977, *6* (2), 24–30.

Salk, Lee. On the custody rights of fathers in divorce. *Journal of Clinical Child Psychology,* 1977, *6* (2), 49–50.

Satir, Virginia. *Peoplemaking*. Palo Alto, Cal.: Science and Behavior Books, 1972.

Seagul, Arthur A., and Seagul, Elizabeth. The noncustodial father's relationship to his child: conflicts and solutions. *Journal of Clinical Child Psychology*, 1977, *6* (2), 11–15.

Selvini Palazzoli, Mara et al. *Paradox and counterparadox*. New York: Jason Aronson, 1978.

Stierlin, Helm. A family perspective on adolescent runaways. *Archives of General Psychiatry*, 1973, *29*, 56–62.

_____. The dynamics of owning and disowning: psychoanalytic and family perspectives. *Family Process*, 1976, *15*, 277–288.

_____. *Psychoanalysis and family therapy*. New York: Jason Aronson, 1977.

Sullivan, Harry Stack. *Conceptions of modern psychiatry*. New York: W. W. Norton, 1940.

_____. *The interpersonal theory of psychiatry*. New York: W. W. Norton, 1953.

Tessman, Lora Heims. *Children of parting parents*. New York: Jason Aronson, 1978.

Thies, Jill Matthews. Beyond divorce: the impact of remarriage on children. *Journal of Clinical Child Psychology*, 1977, *6* (2), 59–61.

Wallerstein, Judith S., and Kelly, Joan B. The effects of parental divorce: adolescent experience. In A. Koupernik (ed.), *The child in his family*. New York: John Wiley and Sons, 1974a.

_____. The effect of parental divorce: experiences of the preschool child. *Journal of the American Academy of Child Psychiatry*, 1974b, *14*, 600–616.

_____. The effects of parental divorce: experiences of the child in early latency. *American Journal of Orthopsychiatry*, 1976a, *46*, 20–42.

_____. The effects of parental divorce: experiences of the child in later latency. *American Journal of Orthopsychiatry*, 1976b, *46*, 256–269.

Weakland, John. Communication theory and clinical change. In P. Guerin (ed.), *Family therapy: theory and practice*. New York: Gardner Press, 1976.

Weiss, Warren W., and Collada, Henry B. Conciliation counseling: the court's effective mechanism for resolving visitation and custody disputes. *The Family Coordinator*, 1977, *26*, 444–446.

INDEX

213